I0820645

CONTINUITY

LIFE BEYOND THE CREDITS

BY BONNIE CLEVERING

WRITTEN WITH JASON CLEVERING

{ punctuate } PRESS.

Creative Director: Jason Clevering
Editors: Allison Lynn / Alicia Wilcox
Copywriter: Alicia Wilcox
Art Director / Design: Corey Ciszek

Published by Punctuate Press New York.
Manufactured in the United States of America.
Signature Book Printing, www.sbpbooks.com

Minimal edits to images have been made to remove non-essential environmental elements and persons that do not affect the integrity of the image and/or the original intent of the image.

Library of Congress Control Number: 2025939587
ISBN: 979-8-9929569-6-2
ISBN (ebook): 979-8-218-49929-7
First Edition

{ punctuate } PRESS.

TABLE OF CONTENTS

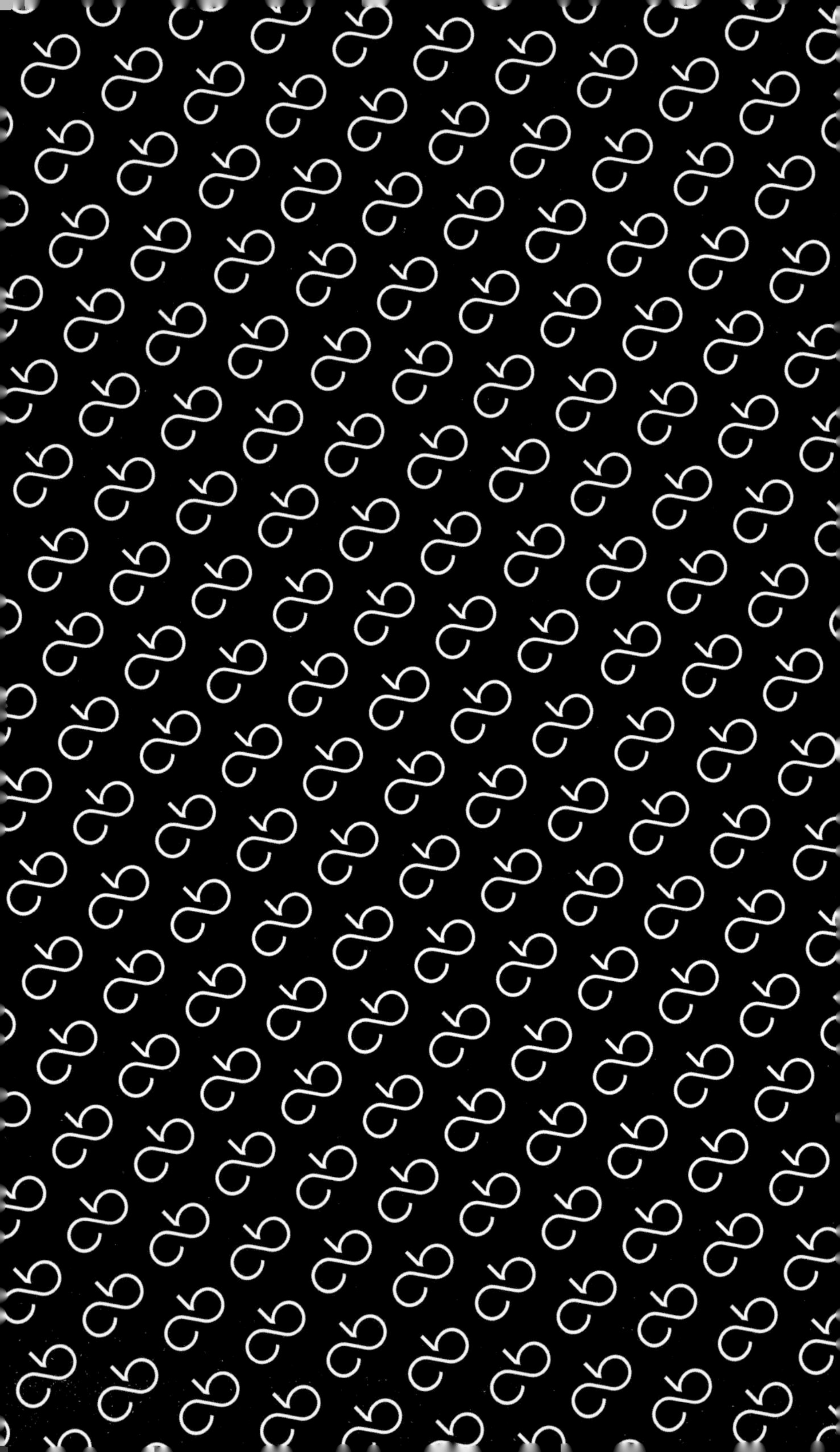

FOREWORD

FIFTY+ YEARS IN THE MAKING

BY JASON CLEVERING, SON

“I’M JUST GLAD SHE’S FINALLY ALL GROWN UP,” I JOKINGLY PROCLAIM WHEN SOMEONE COMPLIMENTS MY MOTHER TO ME.

"I'm just glad she's finally all grown up," I jokingly proclaim when someone compliments my mother to me.

While that comment usually brings a chuckle to anyone within earshot, it wasn't until I began writing my mother's story that I realized the truth in that statement. However strange it may seem, I can honestly say I have watched my mother evolve, mature, and "grow up" right before my very eyes.

I realized at a young age that my mother was different from other mothers. Growing up in a house with walls adorned with photos of famous people with signed phrases that said "Loved making this movie with you" and "Can't wait until our next film" weren't the usual taglines above an autograph that most fans would receive from a celebrity. As a child, huddled in the corner, eavesdropping on the dinner parties my parents threw at their home, I overheard my mom tell stories of working in Hollywood with this actor or director on this film or TV series. I deciphered these as mere party talk, yet I recall the intensity with which people listened to her every word. As a kid in my single digits of years, I don't recall my mom "working" per se. That's not to say she wasn't the busiest person I knew. What I considered "work" for my mom was her dedication to others—mainly to me, my sister, Dana, and after five o'clock, my father.

Even though Dana and I were born in Los Angeles, my mom and dad were quick to pack up the family and move far from "Beverly," "Hills," that is, to the Midwest, where we would be sequestered from the influences of Sunset Boulevard throughout adolescence. Hence why I knew my mother as "Mom" and not a motion picture hair designer; over the years, I have come to understand how difficult the decision to leave a burgeoning career in film behind must have been for her. Still, I also realized through the years that my mom rarely does anything for herself, almost always putting others first. Carting me to the Pinewood Derby replaced touch-ups on set, and whisking Dana across town to ballet classes was the closest Mom got to a chorus line in Indianapolis during the mid-'70s. If there had been a clock that read twenty-four hours a day, my mom would have used every minute down to the second. Her artistic ability, previously reserved for the tresses of Bette Davis and Nancy Sinatra, was now used on class projects, bake sales, and fundraisers that may have raised a few more bucks with the bedazzled banners she made into the wee hours of the night. Her desires were reserved and redirected for attending to family and friends, admittedly of her own decision; she confidently confirmed out loud to newlyweds and first-time mothers how much she enjoyed raising her children and spending vacation days with my dad behind the wheel, road tripping to state fairs or flea markets in small towns without stop lights. As the years passed by, the sunlight strewn into my childhood home began to fade the faces and signatures on those famous photos. However, my mother's memories of her brief time among the stars shone brightly on her face, resounding in her voice every time she told someone about nearly burning Elvis's pompadour to a crisp.

When my sister and I ventured deeper into double-digit birthdays, we relocated to Dallas. Her children now required less supervision, possessed driver's licenses, and could make their own meals. The opportunity for Mom to step back into the limelight came in the way of the film business booming in Texas. In the hierarchy of crew members, she nearly went back to square one on set, attending to extras in crowd scenes on Dallas, spending a few days on a movie of the week, or assisting the head of the hair department on a film a few hours away from home. This allowed her to continue being a mother to her children and a wife to my father. After working sixteen hours, she could still console me between the sobs of a first love lost or roll her eyes on cue when drill team drama shrieked from my sister's mouth. Those movie-making stories that were mere party banter a decade earlier now took on a dash of realism when we would visit her on set. The idols of my childhood, last names like "Cruise" or "Washington," were introduced to me as "Tom" and "Denzel." Sitting in an abandoned director's chair on a set, I was in awe, watching Mom comb a lock of hair into place for the next scene, getting comfortable in her element as she must have been so many years ago. I recall the final day of filming on *Born on the Fourth of July* as Oliver Stone pushed the entire crew past twenty-seven hours of straight filming. Gaffers were taking naps in turns between setups, more than five hundred extras were sleeping on the cold quad steps of Southern Methodist University, and Mom was still going strong, attending to everyone. Throughout all those years of preparing lunches for the next day, tirelessly taking care of us around the clock when we were sick, and waiting up way too late when Dad decided to stay out past his curfew with the boys from the office, my mom's endurance was comparable to that of a triathlete. I watched her that night amidst pyrotechnics and a riot scene get her proverbial legs under her and begin to catch stride back into the dream that she had chased so many years before Dana and I were born. And that smile that was sometimes strained into a slight grin when she had to deal with everything going on with the family was now beaming brightly as an artist.

Strangely enough, a few years later, as a freshman, I was back in that same quad at SMU. Dana was two years behind me before she would be out of the house, but old enough to stay mostly on her own, especially with her brother, twenty-eight miles away from home, in case of an emergency. This allowed my father to begin visiting my mother on location for a couple of weeks at a time, and he slowly started his renewed career as a crew member, doing everything from transportation to the camera department. Eventually, they traveled to work on the same films in cities across America, and we watched my mom and dad go from having marital hierarchy to partners in business, albeit Mom was slightly his senior in resume and birthday. Instead of the family sitting in our living room hearing about the mischievousness of Dan Aykroyd that morning in the makeup chair, we got updates at the end of the day over long-distance phone calls. Our chores went from Dana cleaning up after dinner and me mowing the lawn to us taping every episode each week of *Days of Our Lives* on VHS to send to the set of *Nine Months* so our mother could keep up with Beau and Hope's romance at the irregular watching time of 10 p.m. after filming the mayhem of Robin Williams and Hugh Grant delivering Julianne Moore's make-believe baby. My sister and I were satisfied seeing Mom and Dad work in unison in their marriage. We had grown up seeing them sometimes struggle on separate paths as they tried to make ends meet so that we kids could have every opportunity afforded to a middle-class family. Loud voices behind closed doors had quieted now that they were on a similar path together, and I slightly sighed in relief that, hopefully, those years of disconnect had been soundly defeated. Transversing my twenties and edging near a third decade on the planet, my mother began maturing as mother and wife, colleague and mentor, and everything finally looked like somewhere over the rainbow for the Clevering family as the credits began to roll one after another for Mom.

Blessings being counted a bit too soon, tragedy struck on a fateful Sunday morning in May of 1997. Mom and Dad had moved back to Los Angeles in the mid-‘90s because most of the films they worked on were either shot in California or some portion of the production filmed in Hollywood. With me at the University of Southern California and Dana moving through her master's in psychology in Pasadena, the entire family living on the shore of the Pacific Ocean made sense from every angle. Dad hadn't been feeling well for a few weeks, and we chalked it up to the fact that he had worked on two movies back-to-back: *The Mask*, with Jim Carey, and *Kiss the Girls*, starring Morgan Freeman. Both films were primarily shot at night, and in production terms, that meant going to work in the opposite direction of rush hour traffic in the afternoon and back home in the morning. Even though he was exhausted from that schedule six days a week for nearly nine months, the noise of everyone else going about their day made it difficult to sleep soundly. Presumably, his health was suffering from sleeplessness. A Tuesday that should have been like any other started with a phone call asking me to take him to Cedars Sinai. I'd rarely seen my dad bedridden with the flu, always wanting us to perceive him as the pillar of strength, so checking him into the hospital was as frightening for me as it must have been for him. Waiting for test results that never came quickly enough, the doctors, without verified answers, also leaned toward exhaustion. A couple of days later, as my mom and I returned to my dad's bedside after praying for clarity at church, he passed away from late-stage liver cancer, a discovery that no one saw coming. The partner she had walked through most of life with—in various roles such as a father, friend, and filmmaker—could no longer fill those positions. The woman I saw grow into her own as a respected peer in the industry now had to face the fear of making ends meet again and doing it all by herself. Bearing the burden of her own grief and tending to her children's own emotions of losing a loved one, my mother did what she has always done without missing a beat: she endured.

The second act of her life hanging in the balance from the beginning, enduring the challenges of getting herself back on track, my mom saddled up and strode into the final phase of her personal and professional maturity. She welcomed the fear of being alone, dove deeper into her craft, and challenged herself with more productions that tested the utmost extent of her abilities. From 1997 until 2018, Mom amassed many of her career credits and her most rewarding relationships on and off set. She traveled the world to remote locations that most only saw in photos. She bought her own house and her own car. She upgraded her stature as a mother into a matriarch for actors and friends who leaned on her for advice and understanding from the experiences she had endured and overcome her entire life. Dana shared her humble pride in the person she had become as we watched her blossom into an even more influential role model than she had been our whole lives. Confident and emboldened as a well-aged single woman, she recognized her strengths and embraced any weakness she had to evolve with each finished film while extending her compassion and empathy for others at all hours of the day and night.

I often refer to my mother's evolution as a person and professional simply as "Bonnie." The best way I can explain this concept of "Bonnie" is a mixture of superpowers that include a solid shoulder to cry on, ears that hear every word someone speaks in time of need, and hands that, when laid upon the head of an actor sitting in her chair, instill confidence even when reality's ups and downs have crept too deep into the realm of movie make-believe. And now, a few years into retirement, Mom hasn't slowed down one mile an hour, and my sister and I secretly converse regularly about how much she is wearing us both out. While we joke that she will rest when she passes on, I fear that my pine box will be delivered sooner than hers if I keep up the impossible task of keeping up with "Bonnie." I have come to appreciate her constitution, not so much in her career, as that is obvious with a search on IMDB or a scroll through Netflix. Rather, I marvel at her evolution as a woman, not just as her son, but also as a man.

Over the years, when my mother told stories of fluffing the floppy mop of Hugh Grant and knitting Christmas presents on set with Julia Roberts, people within earshot would always ask, "Why don't you write a book?" Without refrain, she always bashfully refused; her priority in her career has been to protect the privacy of the relationships she has developed. This came along with an internalized thought ringing between her ears of "who would want to read about me?" Maybe it was after the thousandth time talking about turning Tim Allen into Santa Claus, or about the time her dog, Weezle, set an entire prison into lockdown during the filming of *Stone* with Ed Norton and Robert

DeNiro that the voice inside her head turned from doubt to decisiveness about telling her tale. Late one night, Mom sat me down at my home in Barcelona and proposed that we write her book together. While she had this newfound confidence in sharing the story of her life and career, I was awash with fear of the responsibility I would have to undertake to convey her words into prose. Here was a woman who had been responsible for telling some of the greatest stories in movie history, whose own story had a supporting cast that everyone on the planet was aware of, and a life philosophy that sought to find a balance between the good, the bad, and the ugly, and she was asking me to turn it all into something worthy of someone buying not just for the pictures, but actually for the reading.

I knew the number one rule for writing her story before we began typing a single letter. This had been ingrained in our family, and anyone who tried to bend this rule was quickly ushered out. Her motherly instinct has been to shield her "clients" from the stalking wannabes that vulture in for a piece of anything that might be shared as an inflated recollection of hanging out with a celebrity or sold as an incident to the twists of the tabloids. This book was to be *her* story about life beyond the credits, with a glimpse behind the scenes of a search by the characters in her life and career to find normalcy in an industry far from normal. After all, there are plenty of tell-alls on the magazine racks at the end of the check-out conveyor in supermarkets all over the globe. Her book was going to be the opposite of that. With my help, she would write this book from the perspective of the "Bonnie" she had become today. Throughout the process, I would get to know and understand my mother in ways a son rarely has the opportunity to, and in turn, we would develop a deeper understanding of each other.

Our writing began with her sharing life stories each night, some that I knew and others she had kept to herself, as if fearing they might alter my perception of the woman I had put on a pedestal during my younger years. As her son and a writer, I learned much more about her as a mother and a woman. It was enlightening to my upbringing and educational to my future life approach. We laughed a lot and cried a little more, but through it all, we wrote more than just a book together. Through the experience of writing these words within, we revised our relationship and built upon our friendship. Throughout writing toward the final chapter, we added stories and images to an already hefty anthology of emotions and experiences she shared with many people on and off film sets. This experience has been one of my fondest memories in life. Being able to instill acknowledgment in Mom that her life has culminated in something that has somehow mimicked the movies she made is coupled with a pride in myself that I was bestowed with the honor of immortalizing her life and persona in sentences and phrases for anyone and everyone to enjoy.

After all is said and written, I can say with certainty that now that my mother has effectively finished growing up, I sit front and center, witnessing a coming-of-age story that only gets better with time.

I can only hope that one day, I'll grow up to be a little bit more like "Bonnie."

MOVIES AND MEMORIES

Bonnie Clevering with Michael J. Fox, *Greedy*, 1994

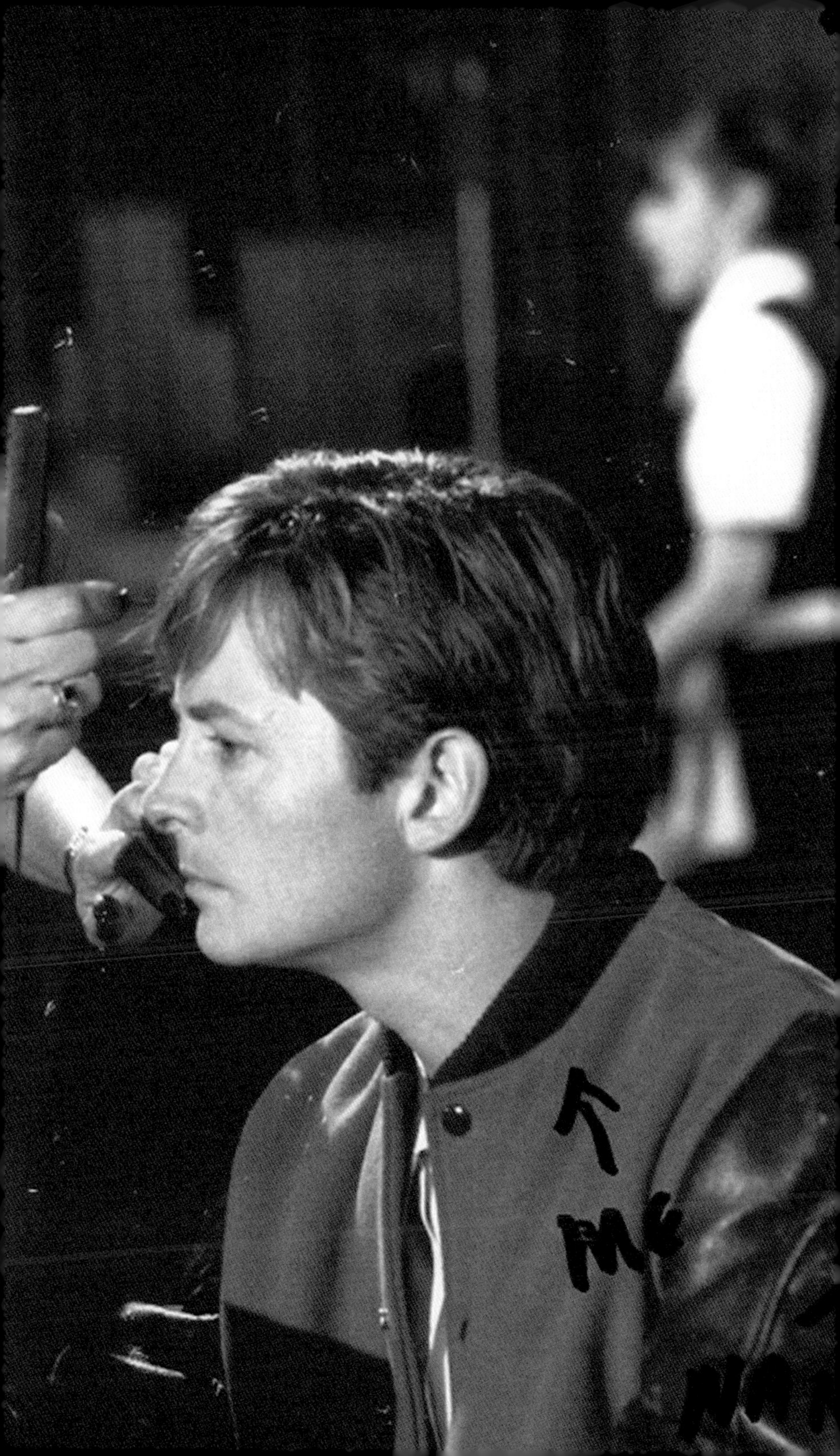
ME

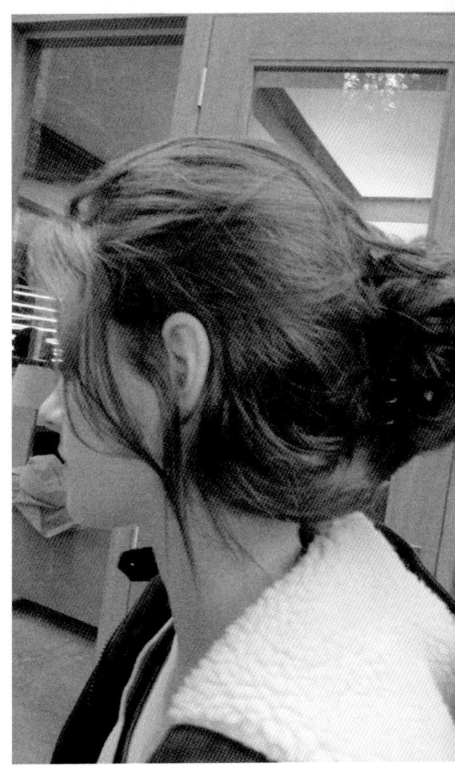

Kristen Stewart,
The Twilight Saga:
Breaking Dawn - Part 2, 2012

CONTINUITY

[CON·TI·NU·I·TY]

1. THE STATE OR QUALITY OF BEING CONTINUOUS.
2. A CONTINUOUS OR CONNECTED WHOLE.
3. A MOTION-PICTURE SCENARIO GIVING THE COMPLETE ACTION, SCENES, ETC., IN DETAIL AND IN THE ORDER IN WHICH THEY ARE TO BE SHOWN ON SCREEN.

The greatest movies of our time all stem from non-linear histories of a screenplay. Scenes are shot out of sequence and then put back into order to become the final story we witness on screen. This is done to accommodate altering times of day, seasons of the year, locations, and actors' schedules.

To maintain this continuity and avoid visuals that fail to link, a hair designer takes four to five photos of the hairstyle for each scene. These "continuity photographs" ensure that the second part of a scene looks like the first part, even if filmed days or weeks apart.

The continuity photographs within this book are in a class of their own in that they are three-dimensional in perception. At first glance, you'll see the celebrity. With a second look, you'll see their character. After a third viewing, the subject's true personality begins to shine in every subsequent Polaroid. The silly faces shared among friends, the goofy glances on set, and the serene smiles to me behind the lens that say, "We're in this together."

Most of my admiration for people in my life is not because of what they have achieved with an Oscar, Emmy, or Grammy, but because of how they continuously brought the infinite loop of continuity back to the center with ease. This has been the most crucial lesson practiced—not perfected, but ultimately learned and utilized as often as possible. The continuity photos in this book form the archive of bonds I created beyond the credits.

Throughout the book, you will see that continuity polaroids from *Erin Brockovich* are highlighted at the beginning of every chapter. This is not because they are the most interesting or happen to have one of the biggest film icons in the frame. The reason is that the film, the character, and the journey endured are the most accurate representations of my self-discovered philosophy of continuity.

Erin constantly navigated the infinite loop of continuity, balancing moments of her life that ebbed and flowed from triumphs and tribulations. Her decisions throughout her story had nothing short of a ripple effect, impacting all aspects of her life and career. If she focused on the families of Hinckley to help them fight their grievances against PG&E, her family felt neglected and ignored. When she felt proud of herself for the first time because what she was doing mattered to others, her blossoming romantic relationship with George wilted. This striving for balance in everything evolving throughout the movie is a prime example of the continuity we strive to maintain.

This ongoing quest for continuity requires everlasting leaps of faith into the unknown. That is why the *Erin Brockovich* polaroids also represent a pivotal moment in many of the lives that contributed to the making of the movie, mine included. For Steven Soderbergh, the film would catapult him from an indie nomad to a film auteur on a global stage. Julia Roberts took the ultimate chance and departed from the safety of a genre of films that had made her America's sweetheart, showing everyone her immense talent with a performance more than worthy of an Oscar. For me, the film brought balance in the continuity of my life after my husband passed away, giving me the confidence to stride through life as an independent woman able to finally lean on my ability to provide for myself, cultivate relationships of my own, develop my craft, and amass years of memories with many film credits beyond the days of working in the glow of *Erin Brockovich*.

THERE ARE TWO SIDES
TO EVERYTHING:
HEADS AND TAILS,
HE SAID, SHE SAID,
HEAVEN AND HELL,
TRUTHS AND LIES,
THE MOON, BEDS, AND
MOST PEOPLE.

SAYING NO TO THE KING

FADE IN:

Perched on a hill separating Los Angeles from the San Fernando Valley sits a modern icon of the theory of "two sides to everything." Millions of people drive past it every day, yet few pause to gaze at it as they do, say, the Eiffel Tower, Big Ben, or Taj Mahal. After all, it is an icon of the city, a defining landmark of the United States, and a historical reminder of legends. It was not built centuries ago, nor was it a gift from an emperor, and it never has had to endure the effects of enemy bombardment—at least in reality. Yet, it stands as a symbol of kings and queens, artists and writers, tragedy and success, and the history of people, places, and memories that encompass the history of Earth.

There's no admission fee to witness this monument. You can't even approach it without the LAPD mobilizing a helicopter and SWAT team to apprehend the daring tourist who isn't content with the two hundred photos they've taken lying next to every star on the Walk of Fame. It was once four letters longer, originally intended to represent a humble housing project that never materialized and lacks doors, windows, or protective walls. Yet, it seems to preserve and protect everything around it, visible and invisible, leaving its mark on an ideology both revered and reviled by millions.

As is true with most things in life, you usually only see one side, and in this case, the adage could not be more significant. There is a glistening white side, bright and bold, beaming in the warm glow of the Southern California sun, a beacon of hopes and dreams come true. It is close enough for one to view but just out of grasp. No matter what time of day or night you see it, and at any angle, it looks as if it is staring back at you, inviting your wants and desires. Although you have never met, it shares memories that can bring you to tears, either of sadness or joy, and sometimes both at the same time. But the dingy aluminum on the other side of its facade also exists, cloaked in darkness, rusted support beams stabbed into the ground, keeping its structure upright when the earth below shakes violently, and its shadow keeps flowers from blooming. At the same time, a cold breeze shrills through the maze of tension wires twisting violently.

However, it takes two sides of this metaphor on stilts to keep the balance of what it represents: a delicate teetering between has and has been, reality and make-believe, one-way and round-trip, fame and obscurity. It defines simplicity and decadence in one word, a line in the sand between what we accept as real life and what we envision as a fairy tale: the Hollywood Sign.

It is a headline that sums up almost everything most people believe about the movie business. It is a mantra that for every celebrity who shines, there is the heartbroken thespian who climbs aboard a Greyhound bus bound for somewhere else east of Universal Studios. It is also the promise that for everyone boarding that bus with shattered realities, a handful of hopefuls cascade down its gum-ridden stairs into the grasp of hopeful possibilities. There has been and always will be the in-your-face side of Hollywood and

IT IS A HEADLINE ALMOST EVERYTHING ABOUT THE

THAT SUMS UP
MOST PEOPLE BELIEVE
MOVIE BUSINESS.

the locked doors that have everybody searching for the key, letting a select few into its seclusion. The ability to obtain notoriety and fortune seems simple, but that promise has as much probability of fruition as a mechanical rabbit being caught at the dog race. Every day, millions of people wake up and stare at that sign, trying to decipher its code, the secret formula for success in show business. It is as if those who have made it onto the posters and into the credits have been born into it through bloodlines; sometimes, they are. But, some fight tooth and nail, perfecting their craft. Over time and even more time, with much hard work and a bit of luck, a few are invited into the kingdom and bestowed with titles such as actor, director, producer, or any other with a union affiliation. Even hairstylists are adorned with the grandeur of nobility.

I still look back on the past five decades and try to figure out how I ended up with a chance to mingle among entertainment aristocracy. From the beginning, I hoped nobody would recognize me as an outsider. After all, being raised by parents who owned a small grocery market in Illinois did not give me any knowledge of the Pacific ruling class. As much as I hoped the fake gold sticker of the State seal meant more, my cosmetology license was not stamped with a regal crest. No, I was saying novenas and practicing pin curls in the hopes that someone I had seen in TV Guide would stumble into a salon I was working at off the beaten path where I would give them the perfectly bubbled beehive. Then they would sweep me into their convertible, through the MGM gates, and into happily ever after—a film-worthy fairytale that nearly never happens.

My husband and I were married a few days before we left Ft. Lauderdale, Florida for the furthest point west: Los Angeles. He suffered from a rare blood ailment that made it

I WAS SILENT. I WAS PENSIVE AND CONFLICTED, BUT I HAD MADE UP MY MIND FROM THE MOMENT I SPOKE INSIDE THE EXPANSE OF THAT ROOM, THE ECHO OF MY WORDS STILL LINGERING IN MY MIND.

---

difficult for him to clot, and a pulled tooth two days before our departure ensured that our drive would trade sightseeing for stitches in a dozen differently decorated emergency rooms along the way. With little money and a blue Pontiac, visions of America's fantasyland swam through our heads as we waited a few days later, in a sea of traffic, for our turn to exit off the freeway where Sunset Boulevard beckoned.

We moved into a small apartment in Glendale at the base of the San Fernando Mountains. In exchange for rent, we managed the small complex. I sat down at our kitchenette each morning, thumbing through trade magazines, searching for any film or television production that would give a newly minted hairstylist a chance. A lucky break in the form of a friend of a friend led to lunch with another friend, and that person made a call that gave me a chance to start working at Hollywood Center Studios. I did whatever they told me to do, from setting wigs to curling the blonde ringlets of chorus dancers. One day, while cleaning my brushes, I heard word that Larry Germain was searching for an apprentice to assist him personally at Universal Studios. Since beauty artists are rarely spoken of in the mainstream media, you may have no idea who Larry Germain was, but at that time, he was the Musk, Zuckerberg, and Jobs of Hollywood hairstyling.

It was a perfect spring day in Burbank, as it is almost every day in Burbank. I had spent hours doing my hair,

John Wayne, Ensenada, 1966

selecting the ideal dress—not too casual or sexy. I did not want him to feel I was hopeless, and I did not want to send the wrong message, regardless of his sexual orientation. It was the first and last day I ever chose a preferred work color for the job at hand: black. The color black can be casual and commanding, seductive and selective, and can make you hidden or noticed by the length of a skirt and the number of buttons fastened. Most importantly, black lets you sweat without them seeing you sweating, and that morning, I was spewing forth from pores I did not know I possessed.

As I approached the union local, nerves on edge, I glimpsed the line of ladies slithering out onto the sidewalk in the distance, and my knees began to buckle as my hands went limp. I had seen lines of hopeful and desperate actors standing single file, waiting to spout a few lines of screenwriting prose to a lone casting director behind a folding table. Still, the line of perfectly primped, portfolio-toting beauticians wrapping around the building nearly made me turn around and run. Some were practicing handshakes while others were going through the motions of wrapping fifteenth-century hair on imaginary headpieces, much like a lone ballerina practices her audition for *Swan Lake*. I stood at the back of the line and tried not to vomit over my patent leather pumps.

After waiting nearly all day, I entered through the heavy wood office door, parted just enough to let one hopeful soul in and one dashed spirit stumble out.

His voice was the first thing that shook me. "Come in and sit down," he boomed, rattling rafters, *Fiddler on the Roof* meets *The Wizard of Oz*.

Seated at the end of a long table occupied by other

executives, frail in his features, strong in his demeanor, the envy of everyone present, there was Larry Germain. Before my backside met the metal seat, he was already talking about how he did not expect to find someone today, and then he spoke about the greatness of his work and that it would be a privilege for anyone to work with him and on, and on, and on, and on.

Suddenly, he stopped short and asked me, seemingly not caring about what I had to say, "What do you want from this business?"

A deep breath, a forced exhalation, and in the most succinct voice I could muster, with all the sincerity in the world, I responded, "To learn from the best."

There was a moment of silence, a long moment, as we both contemplated what I had just answered. I didn't know if he had heard me or if he was calculating his method of attack. Then, abruptly, without words, he stood. I stood. He shook my hand with both of his, lingering longer than I would have thought necessary, given the length of the line that had formed behind me. I languidly walked out through the gap in the doors, spirit intact, confident that I knew exactly what I wanted from Tinsel Town from that day forth.

The next day and two loads of laundry later, the pre-heat light on the oven clicked off, and the phone rang. I do not know how I knew; I just knew, before I answered, what was in store for me on the other end of the line.

"Hello... Bonnie Clevering," I said with confidence, stern but polite.

"It's Larry Germain. It's yours," he boasted with the whim of a game show host.

I was silent. I was pensive and conflicted, but I had made up my mind from the moment I spoke inside the expanse of that room, the echo of my words still lingering in my mind.

"The apprenticeship. It's yours. I have chosen you to learn from the best," Larry reiterated, his profound tone becoming confused as his voice struggled to convey his proclamation.

Then it came out as if somebody had pulled the string in my back, and the recording played with perfect annunciation: "Thank you, Mr. Germain. It was great meeting you the other day. I do want to learn from the best. Unfortunately, I have not met that person yet. Best of luck in finding your new apprentice."

And, with that, I hung up the phone and put the pot roast in the oven.

At this point, you must think I am absolutely nuts. Trust me, that was not the first or last time; I was likely certifiable for several reasons. I was essentially courted and crowned in a few days, and I cast off the gown and shattered the slippers way before midnight. But I knew that life was full of opportunities, and I did not have to settle for something or someone I thought would make me different from who I was inside and what I wanted from my career that was only just beginning. I slept soundly that night, not from the two bottles of cheap Red Mountain wine that my husband and I shared but from the feeling of control I had over my destiny that day and the decision that I knew would change my life forever.

Months passed, and word had made its rounds from call sheet to call sheet about this woman who had refused the grandeur of opportunity from Larry Germain. This woman, whom no one had heard of, had a resume that no one had seen and credits that had not rolled. I shrewdly lifted a brow each time I heard two girls working three chairs down from me cackle on about the mystery woman and what she must have been thinking. But, as word traveled and the story became more fantastically recanted among circles, there was a familiar anecdote at the end of the conversation: “That woman must have some balls.” Maybe that was metaphorically correct, but it just came down to knowing what I wanted in my career and life, and I wasn’t going to settle for anything different.

So, when the phone rang a few weeks later, I nearly split my polyester pants when I hung up the receiver, jumping across the apartment, flinging open the screen door, and shouting down to my husband, collecting rent across the courtyard.

“It’s the King! It’s the King! I’m going to work on the same set as the King!” I screamed with glee, joyously shaking the balcony railing to its limits. No, he did not have a generational number after his name, and he was not from a foreign land. Rather he was a homegrown, guitar-strumming, hip-swinging music legend adorned with gold records. You guessed right... from his blue suede shoes to his teddy bear, it was the King of Rock and Roll, Elvis Presley.

Having become a union member in Los Angeles, the assignment had been handed down to me to work with

Nancy Sinatra. She had recently been cast in a movie called *Speedway* with Elvis, and she'd told him about me and said that I would be great for the film. A few weeks later, I was coiffing Nancy's silver locks and touching up Elvis's famous pompadour, loving every minute with both of them. From their singing and dancing to the practical jokes played on all of us by The Colonel and the Memphis Mafia, the entire time on that film still ranks among the most memorable months of my life and career. Those days with Elvis and Nancy were life-changing but not career-changing. And what I am about to tell you would make you think I was comfortable in a strait jacket, just like Elvis did one day.

We were nearing the end of filming when the door to the makeup room was flung open late in the afternoon. Mary Keats, the department head at MGM Studios, asked me if I would step outside with her. I stood up quickly and scurried out the door behind Ms. Keats, my mind flipping through my memory bank about what I may or may not have done. The sunshine blinded me momentarily as I nearly tripped over the threshold when she threw open the stage door, her hand waving behind her as she hurried me closer to her stride.

Around the corner and out of sight of the rest of the crew, Mary took a deep breath and exclaimed, "Elvis asked me to make sure that you are on the crew list for every film in his contract at the studio."

Her mouth revealed a smirkier smile with each word she spoke. Her eyes widened as she gazed down at me, a sort of parental approval when reading a better-than-average report card. My mouth was ajar, trying to decipher if my ears heard correctly or perhaps the searing sun played tricks on my mind while I fought to mouth anything audibly comprehensible.

Mary smugly said, “The words you are looking for are ‘yes’ followed by ‘thank you.’” Her arms slowly folded over one another with impatient expectation of my response.

As I stood there, staring at Mary’s tapping patent leather pump, the weight of the decision I had to make felt heavier with each passing second.

I nodded in rhythm with her tapping, my words carefully chosen. “Thank you, but I need the night to consider. I’ll let you know tomorrow.”

Mary’s foot came to a stern stop, her arms dropping heavily to her side. She testily exclaimed, “Tomorrow. The King isn’t used to waiting for an answer.”

Ms. Keats stammered away. As she walked away, my breath caught in my throat, the weight of the decision settling like a lead weight in my stomach.

That night, after talking with my husband while not putting the cork back in the bottle of wine emptied all too quickly, I lay in bed staring at the ceiling fan for most of the moonlit hours. Visions of traveling the world to see exotic lands and meet presidents, maybe even actual royalty, meandered in my mind. I was in awe and disbelief that Elvis Presley wanted me to do every movie with him from that moment on. My husband and I could afford a house, a car with white-wall tires, and maybe even a Cadillac. Everything anyone in my business would want was handed to me on a silver platter and at such an early time in my career. At the same time, the fantasies of the possibilities were playing

Elvis Presley and Nancy Sinatra, *Speedway*, 1968

out in front of my eyes on the stark ceiling; the shadows of doubt were dancing on all four walls.

All I had to do was sign on the dotted line, but I knew there was fine print I had not considered, and I paused to wonder what I was missing. At that moment, I recalled a lesson that had been taught for centuries and continues today, just as my father taught me years ago, one morning while riding in a truck on his milk delivery route. We passed these big houses, looking at the twinkling Christmas lights glistening off the newly fallen snow. I imagined life was perfect in those homes because they all had pillars and a fancy car parked in a circular driveway. I asked my father if that meant that they had everything in life. My father pointed out to me how one had an aunt who was just diagnosed with leukemia, another had divorced because of an affair, and two more had sent sons off to the war and had not heard anything from them for weeks. While those houses may have looked very nice, what my father said next has resonated loudly in my life from that moment onward.

"Money isn't everything, and most of the time, what you want and see is not necessarily what you get."

Standing there on the precipice of my dreams coming true, I realized the actual cost of giving up my personal ambitions if I said yes to Elvis. I would never see my husband, and the kids that we were desperately trying to conceive would never be brought into this world. The joys of holidays with family and friends and all those simple moments worth the weight of gold in my memory bank would never be, and I would regret that forever. As dawn began to scrub the shadows from the room and paint the ceiling in soft golden light, I smiled at my still-sleeping husband and quietly rose to face the music that would play out for me at the studio that day.

About mid-day, sometime between rewinding the song to a choreographed diner scene and coiffing curls on bubbly waitresses, I noticed Mary Keats, side-eye scowling at me, presumably shocked I hadn't run up to her first thing and said "yes" and "thank you."

I took a deep breath, pulled back my shoulders, crossed the sound stage, and without hesitation said, "Ms. Keats, you are aware that Elvis and I have begun to develop a pleasant friendship, so I would appreciate it if I were the one to tell him, but I am going to decline the offer kindly."

I firmly projected forth my hand to shake Mary's hand, her quizzical gaze accented with a misbelieving tilt of her head, somewhat reluctantly shaking my hand and nodding her approval of my request. As Ms. Keats walked away, I scanned the stage to see where Elvis was huddled up with the boys. In one of the red and white glossy booths, he was holding court as usual, rousing laughter from his disciples as he told a story I'm sure was only for the guys to hear. As I approached the group, hushing hands and flushed cheeks confirmed the probable R-rating of the tale being told. Elvis, always the gentleman, immediately leaped to his feet to greet me.

"Hiya, Bonnie," he said, the words leaving his lips almost as slick as the black tuft of hair on his head.

"Hiya, Elvis. Do you mind if I talk to you in private?"

After a few eye rolls and a couple of "uh-ohs," Elvis gently held my elbow and walked me away from the boys, waving his hand behind him to stifle their innuendos. I felt as if I was levitating as Elvis guided me out of the sound stage.

3764 Highway 51 S
Memphis Tenn

LOS ANGELES. CALIF.
PM
30 NOV
1967
58

Thank You

Dear Bonnie
Elvis and I want to thank you for the beautiful silver set I know our "Little one" will get a lot of use from it We do appreciate your thoughtfulness
Priscilla

The relentless heat that had plagued the other side of the hill from Hollywood had me practically fainting, or maybe my nerves were starting to get the best of me. My eyes pulled into focus, and the kind gaze of the man I had idolized as a teen now staring at me as a colleague quickly calmed me into composure.

"Elvis, I can't tell you how honored I am to be allowed to work with you on all your movies," the timbre of my voice wavering into weakness, standing a little more upright to conjure confidence as I finished my sentence. "But if I say yes to what surely would be a dream come true, I will also have to say goodbye to my life as my own."

Realizing the outcome before I vocalized my final thoughts, Elvis held both of my hands, a slight squeeze encouraging me to continue.

"And I just have too many other things I want to experience with my family to leave them all behind."

Elvis grasped my hands a little tighter, acknowledging he knew what I meant as we had talked enough about family and friends before. After all, years before, he had given up most of what I was not ready to leave behind, and in retrospect, he would spend most of his life trying to get even a small sum of it back.

Dropping my hands, he wrapped his arms around me, exhaling with a heavy sigh; he whispered, "I wish I would have said 'no' to a few more people, a few more times in my life."

It was then that I understood that being bestowed a title of royalty must mean your life is not necessarily your own, and

I sank deeper into his embrace. Languidly breaking apart, we headed back inside and silently went our separate directions. I paused a few steps later, straightened my appearance, and returned to work, raising Nancy's bouffant just a bit higher.

Elvis and I kept in contact a few times over the years, and I realized the compromises that seem like they will make everything easier and better are not always the best to make. Those decisions that take away what you want from life will eventually take their toll, and one day, you will look back and wonder how you got where you are without all the memories in life that are truly priceless. Saying no to the King afforded me many wonderful years with my family, two kids, many friends, and holidays celebrated with siblings.

One August night in 1977, my family and I were sitting in our car outside a Kiwanis Club in Indianapolis, Indiana when an announcer interrupted a Bee Gees song with the news that Elvis had passed away. In that moment, between the tears, I recalled that special hug from the man I knew as a friend who had given me the chance to follow my dreams, his voice still echoing in my mind the words he whispered to me all those years ago.

MUFFLING MY SOBS, I LOOKED IN THE REARVIEW MIRROR AT MY TWO CHILDREN ASLEEP IN THE BACKSEAT, LAID MY HEAD ON MY HUSBAND'S SHOULDER, AND THOUGHT, MAYBE IF ELVIS HAD BEEN GIVEN A CHOICE OF SAYING NO, WE ALL COULD HAVE HEARD A FEW MORE SONGS SUNG BY THE KING.

6/1/99

Red Bobby Pin each Side

Sc105 D15
Linwood Barn (cows)
Sc107 D15 Ambrosino Living Room

02 THE TRAILER AND THE CHAIR

SOME MIGHT DESCRIBE
IT AS A PSYCHIATRIST'S
COUCH, OTHERS AN
EXAMINATION TABLE,
AND IT EVEN SERVED
AS A THRONE UPON WHICH
A HOUSEMAID WAS
MAGICALLY TRANSFORMED
INTO A FAIRYTALE PRINCESS.

Bonnie
HAIR

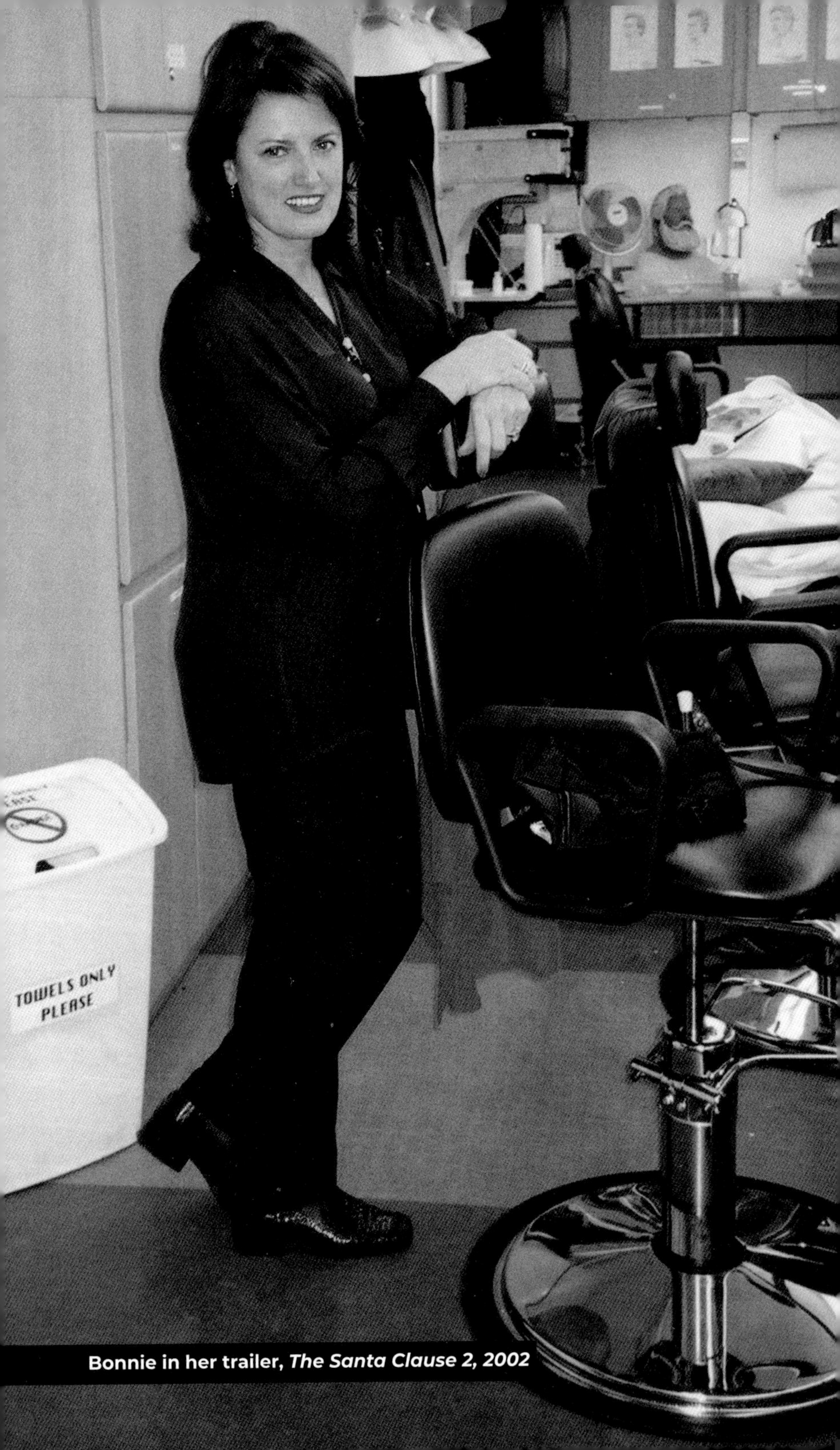

Bonnie in her trailer, *The Santa Clause 2*, 2002

I've sipped champagne on private planes, stayed in luxury villas, dined with elites, and lived a significant portion of my life in a six-by-twenty-foot trailer.

It's as generic as a trailer can be, nothing special. Blonde parquet cabinets lining one side, scuffed linoleum flooring, and a wall of mirrors surrounded by forty IKEA light bulbs. Sure, I try to make it a little more personal with a few snapshots of family and friends, pets, and the random quote clipped out of a magazine I glanced through in between takes sitting in a steel mill made to look like a Manhattan penthouse in the middle of Pittsburgh. The bathroom in the trailer is tiny, without a shower and with a non-functioning toilet. This room stores shampoo and conditioner, styling products, dozens of water bottles, and shipping cases that have traveled more than most people around the world.

Sometimes, music is playing and people are singing—and the Macarena has been danced on more than a few occasions. There are secrets whispered behind closed doors, arguments that shudder the suspension, and often laughter that spills from the open windows and funnels through the maze of similar trailers nearby. Even though the walls are thin and the door hinges barely catch, this trailer has

EVEN THOUGH THE WALLS ARE THIN AND THE DOOR HINGES BARELY CATCH, THIS TRAILER HAS A SENSE OF SAFETY.

---

a sense of safety. So much so that emotions are protected from the outside world, and when tears flow, and private joys come forth, there is the sense that this is the only space in the world that will contain and protect everything said, felt, and shared.

In this trailer is one crucial piece of furniture: my chair. It is made of shiny metal and foam, black worn pleather, and a footrest placed just so that it fits nearly any leg length. It goes up and down and swivels around. This chair is comfortable, but not so much that you would want to sleep in it, although, on many occasions, I have contorted my body in it at three in the morning, hoping to find one position or another for a power nap. It is the single most important location on a film set. It can erase tears, spark joy, and wipe away the emotional contents of an email that remain even after it has been deleted. My chair helps relieve tension from a fight the night before and builds strength when the toll of a relationship has stripped the fortitude from every muscle in the body. There is no manual for the operation of this chair, and I have had to learn its abilities and weaknesses, as well as the unique language it speaks, so that when someone sits down, my chair and I can work together to transform the reality of the person into the illusion of the character.

Through the years, I have tried to define my chair. A styling tool and beauty instrument of sorts, my chair is so much more. Some might describe it as a psychiatrist's couch, others an examination table, and it even served as a throne upon which a housemaid was magically transformed into a fairytale princess. Although some would call me crazy for several other reasons, the fact that I look at my chair as an animate object would rightfully get me committed if I spoke of it that way in certain social circles. But, without a doubt, that chair has a life of its own. The arms wrap around you and cradle you when the exhaustion of filming six days a week for three months has taken its toll. While

Al Pacino, *Insomnia*, 2002

thin and cold, those arms are strong and supportive and hold you up when the world seems to have let you down.

No matter where my trailer is parked, in a field or a studio lot, it is the epicenter of any film production. It has a companion, usually not so far away, that cooks over three hundred meals a day, and the two have a love/hate relationship at times, depending on the menu of the day and whether tequila has been consumed the night before. While many may argue that the director or actors, producers,

Barbara Hershey and Keanu Reeves,
***Tune in Tomorrow*, 1990**

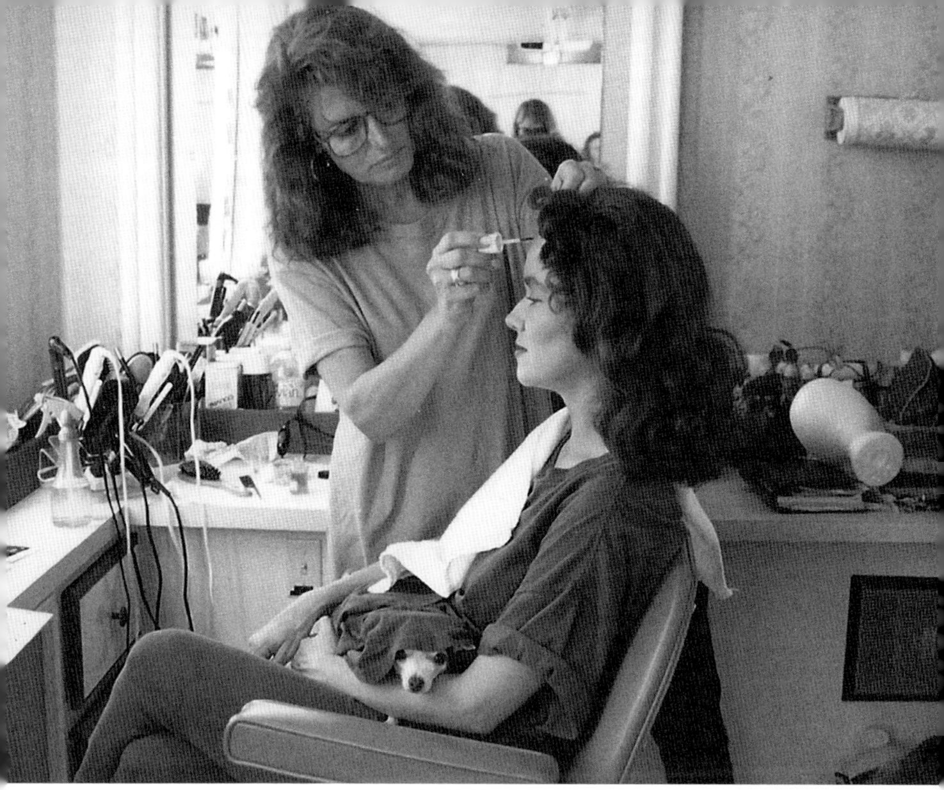

and sometimes the writers are the most important people on the set, I, most of the time, beg to differ, with all due respect. Outside of the actual production elements of a film that an audience sees in a multiplex, in the opinion of many in my business, the two most influential groups of people on any movie set are the caterers and the beauty artists.

After months and sometimes years of preparing to film a movie, countless rewrites of a script, financing that falls through and is resolved at the last moment, along with cast schedules and more rewrites, this small handful of people in catering and hairstyling in many ways have the collective ability to determine whether a movie is a box office flop or an Academy Award nominee. This ability to alter the fate of a film is something I have never used or abused. Likewise, I have never personally wished for a production to dwindle into a heap of worthless celluloid.

How are these individuals with seemingly the least important jobs on a movie set bestowed with such control over its fate? After all, our credits do not fade in at the beginning of the movie but rather scroll up in a rapid blur, usually after the seat bottoms have sprung into their folded position and the ushers have begun sweeping un-popped corn kernels and squished Milk Duds from the sticky cinema floor. It is quite elementary in explanation and makes all the sense in the world when revealed.

The concept originates from the caterer's influence on a film set over the entire crew, the cast, the interns who are compensated with a meal, and even the extras who have to endure various production difficulties. It can easily be explained from a common childhood experience. I recall going to elementary school each day as a youth in Aurora, Illinois. During first period, my classmates and I all looked like chickens with our heads cut off as we darted below the lifted lids of our desktops only to spring forth on cue as the static cleared, the bell tones chimed, and the assistant principal's voice crackled on the speaker mounted near the door. It was the morning reading of the lunch menu. We all had visions of roasted turkey steaming next to the buttered fluff of mashed potatoes, a double cheeseburger with slightly salted fries, and a warm peach cobbler slowly melting a scoop of vanilla bean ice cream.

Instead, the dreaded words screeched forth as if the Wicked Witch of the West were sealing our fate from a thatched hut: Salisbury steak with mushroom gravy,

---

IT IS IMPORTANT THAT EACH OF US HAS OUR OWN TRAILER AND CHAIR. THESE PLACES AND RETREATS ARE WHAT ALLOW US TO EMBRACE HUMILITY AS A PART OF OUR CONSTITUTION.

---

asparagus, fruitcake, and homogenized milk. The thought of what is supposed to be one of the daily highlights of any child's early learning experience turned into a dreaded hour crammed between geography and math. While the thoughts of revolution reverberated through the halls with the furious slamming of locker doors, my pent-up anger seemed to have an auditory effect that made me fail to hear most of what was taught in the half hour before and after lunch. To this day, I am somewhat convinced this is why boys and girls refrain from interaction until their double-digit years: because of the fear of an uncontrollable bodily function sounding out at the most inappropriate time or that mushroom gravy seeps through skin pores during P.E.

Tim Allen, *The Santa Clause 2*, 2002

Now, let us fast-forward this entire scenario to even bigger kids, such as the ones found on a movie set in the form of directors, actors, camera operators, union drivers, and hair stylists. Imagine the Salisbury steak episode but with limp shrimp scampi, charred filet mignon, and cold, runny crème brûlée. If lunchtime was the highlight of my day as a fourth grader, it is the crown jewel in the production schedule of a exhausted, overworked teamster. A bad caterer is the kiss of death for any film. Once the crew must resort to ham sandwiches and granola bars from the craft service table, you can rest assured that the blockbuster potential of a movie has fizzled into the cosmos of nothingness. However, when you put together a bunch of short-order chefs capable of Michelin Star cuisine in a doublewide trailer with top-of-the-line kitchen appliances, the culinary à la carte menu they provide to salivating satisfaction can even help turn a script like *Office Space* into a cinematic classic.

Fortunately or not, the other third of the production weight falls flat on top of the beauty trailer and into my hands. So, how does a hair stylist have any control over the success of a film that costs millions of dollars and employs a crew of hundreds of people or more? In essence, I am not just a hairstylist. While I hold neither educational degrees nor doctorates, my knowledge comes from a more profound, observant institution. For decades, I have seen ordinary or somewhat ordinary people come into my trailer and emerge in an hour or so as a completely different person. Once, I even saw a man walk in and sit down, and three hours later, Santa Claus got up from my chair and stepped out into the Southern California sun. On cue, I have seen extreme anguish pour out of a child playing with her pink Barbie Corvette moments earlier. And I have witnessed a grown man nervously fidgeting over a text message he just received from a spouse, put down the device, and moments later fling

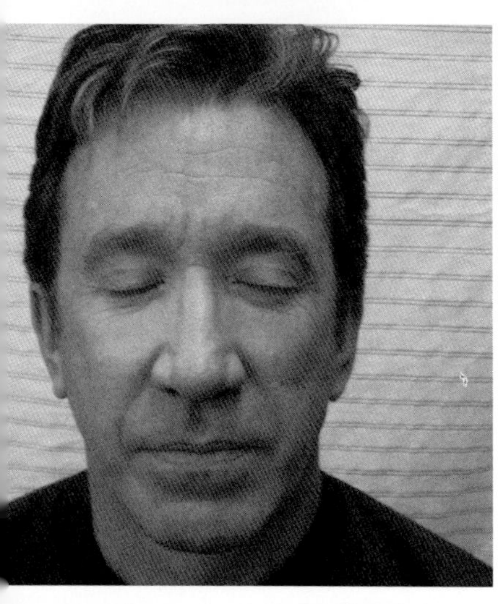

Tim Allen, *The Santa Clause 2*, 2002

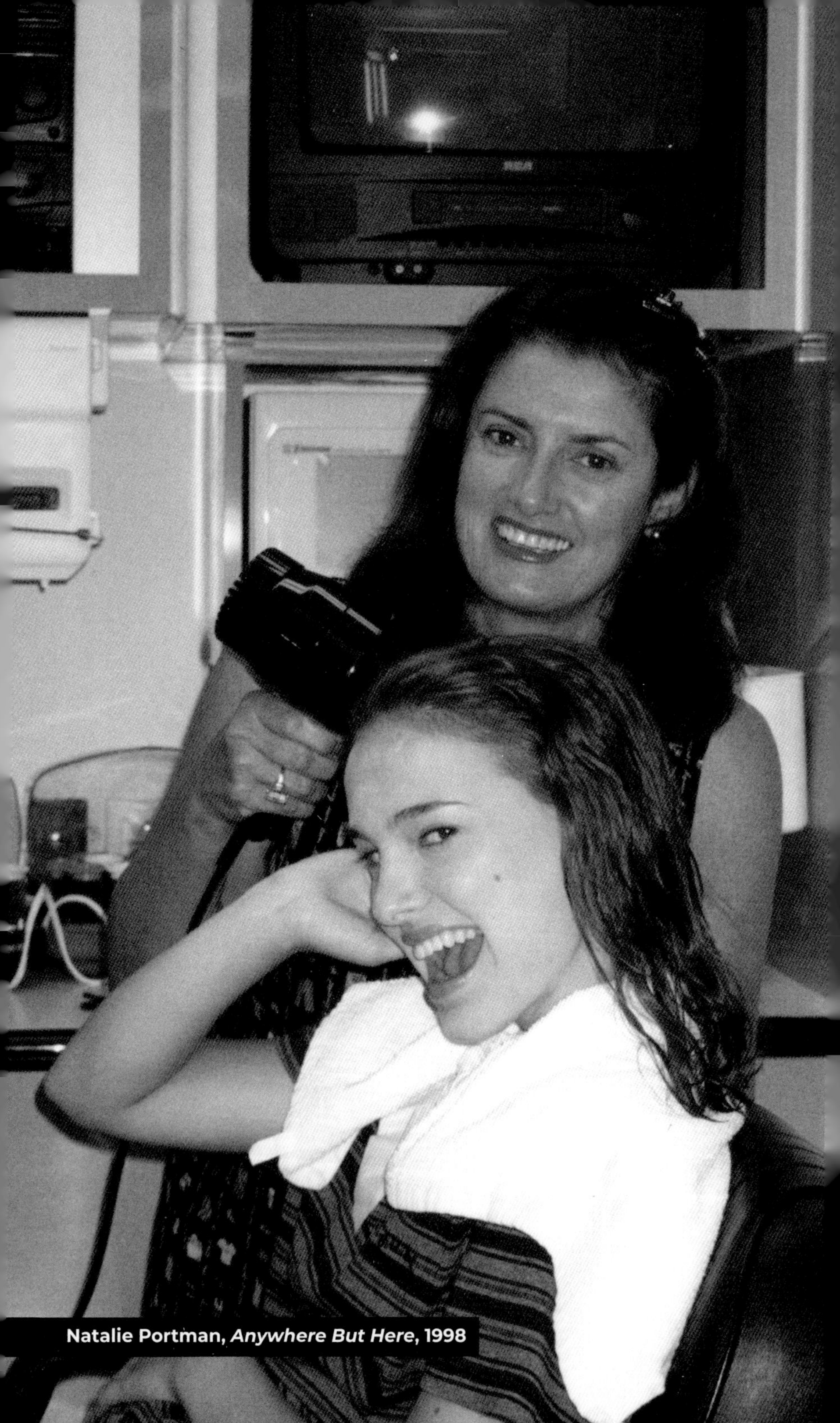

Natalie Portman, *Anywhere But Here*, 1998

himself in front of twenty stunt performers firing machine guns. After working on over one hundred films and television productions, I feel I am qualified with a unique perspective on the human condition. I have privately awarded myself honors in psychiatry, psychology, and sociology and excelled in knowledge of romantic relationships.

As a hairstylist, I must be an extraordinary listener, even when I have heard the same tale of woe from the same actress' mouth every morning at 6:15 a.m. for the past two months. My shoulders are strong but with enough cushion to console the hardest of tears. My eyes are soft and deep to allow hearts and souls in with friendship without getting lost in pity. My hands are gentle, yet have a confidence that lets you know you are safe while we pull on the wig that will transform you from the regular human being who just lost a loved one into an action hero who saves the planet.

Although I hold no professional credentials as a therapist, healer, or any other such profession, when an actor enters my trailer with a mental suitcase packed full of life's harsh realities, the heavy emotional baggage evident in their disheveled hair and exhausted eyes, I need to be whatever they need to ease their burden. If I don't, the chances of a successful day of shooting are all but lost, and the burden gets passed to the unsuspecting crew, who will bear the brunt of the beast that emerges in the form of a forty-something throwing tantrums like the worst of any kindergarten class. If I fail, there is no level of special effects or editing tricks that can cover the real-life emotional strain when it is projected on an IMAX screen under the microscopic glare of the judgmental public eye.

Over the years, I have strived to perfect my craft. Sometimes, the elasticity of a curl eludes me. In some weather situations, it is as if I am battling the gods to keep a finger wave from unraveling into a bird's nest perched on the brow of a two-time Academy Award winner. But after all this time, I finally got this hairstyling thing down. I may "just" be a hairstylist, but my expertise and passion for hair are unmatched. It is neither rocket science nor brain surgery, although the outcomes of a simple cut and blow-dry could have life-altering emotional effects. There are thousands and thousands of us out there. Some just cut hair; others are colorists who can take the bright orange mistake of one and replace the wedding-morning horror with waves of golden locks, seemingly windswept, as the beaming bride walks down the aisle. Some of us have perfected the permanent wave in mini-mall salons across the country, and others transform slender Amazons into catwalk creatures of majesty that fill the pages of fashion magazines around the world every month.

So, what makes me different than everybody else out there with a cosmetology license taped to a salon mirror? It comes down to choices and luck, and I mean lots of luck. Not to mention timing, patience, and a bit more luck. In reality, the answer is simple: humility. I have held back sheer joy when others around me were miserable, and I have run as fast as my little legs could carry me to hide behind a tree and cry so that I would not ruin the creative joy of fifty people who worked three hours pulling off the perfect Steadi-Cam shot after twenty takes. When the realm of Hollywood seems as if it is spinning off its axis into the darkness of space, I have to be humble and put others before myself. When I'm feeling shaken because I've just lost my husband to cancer, I find a way to steady my hands and use them to comfort one of the world's biggest celebrities, helping to wash away their anger and turmoil as they go through an impending divorce.

I have learned to utilize my humility on a movie set and

in every aspect of my life. I've learned that humility is the key to lasting friendships and building a functional family in which children and adults realize the solutions to their emotions on their own so that I was not at risk of misguiding them and ultimately being blamed. But, with this humility, there is an accompanying risk of forgoing my sanity to protect another person's feelings. There is a danger of letting my emotions build inside until they begin to physically take their toll, or worse, explode at an unforeseen moment with words and actions that are hard to repair in any relationship. That is why, when I need to release my feelings without the fear of dropping an emotional time bomb, I always have my trailer and my chair nearby. Of course, I do not literally take my trailer and chair everywhere with me, as they won't fit in a motel room in Barstow or first-class from JFK to LAX. My trailer and chair are simple places in my surroundings where I can always find seclusion and a safe place to release my emotions. It may be the shade of a tree and a rolling case to sit on, away from the eyes and ears of microphones and cameras capturing everything that moves. Or it could be my car with the seat warmer on, rolling through the winding roads of Mulholland Drive in January, listening to a Johnny Mathis song that brings back memories of happier times even though I was just belittled and chewed out by a legendary actress with a snide smirk because she thought I was not capable of flat ironing her hair.

We all must have our own trailer and chair. These retreats allow us to accept humility as a part of our constitution. And we should always be aware of where this special place is and what it contains, making it our own with whatever fosters peace and awareness. It may be an area of the house with a loveseat near the window, looking out on your favorite tree. It could be a dressing table with everything that makes you look and feel beautiful, ready and waiting within arm's reach, or a bench outside your favorite cafe, holding a cup of tea

Martin Short and Kurt Russell, *Captain Ron*, 1992

that warms your hands and soul. Wherever your trailer and chair may be, it should be somewhere you feel safe to release and face your emotions, alone or with a trusted listener. This listener should be humble and without self-importance when you need their eyes, arms, shoulders, and hands. My ability to listen, calm with my hands, lend a shoulder to cry on, and hug with strength or softness in my arms is my true talent, both inside and outside the trailer. This was my distinguishing ability from all the other millions of hair stylists around the world who are equally or even better at using shears and styling tools in salons and on fashion shoots. I firmly believe that my instincts and abilities to comfort and empower actors, helping them to break out of their shells and become the believable characters that audiences see on the screen, are what allowed me to reach the pinnacle of my craft and industry.

I always looked forward to seeing my trailer on the first day I started a new film. That stark white exterior shone in the early light, with wood wedges beneath its wheels to keep it steady as I climbed the stairs, creaked open the door, and sat in my chair. At that moment, with all the fear and anxiety that I always felt starting a new show, I knew that no matter how tough it got, both on or off the set, this production had a good chance of making it. Everyone who entered and exited would have shared in my humility, whether they knew it or not.

AFTER THAT, I WOULD TAKE A DEEP BREATH, CLOSE MY EYES, SAY A LITTLE PRAYER, AND HOPE THE CATERER COULD MAKE A DECENT BREAKFAST BURRITO.

03 THE JOURNEY

OLD ITALIAN WIVES' TALE:

RUBBING THE HANDS ON THE STOMACH OF A WOMAN WHO WAS ABOUT TO GIVE BIRTH WOULD GIVE LUCK TO ANOTHER WOMAN, BASICALLY GUARANTEEING CONCEPTION.

11 2017 07 07 0001 AB 2 5 Obstetric

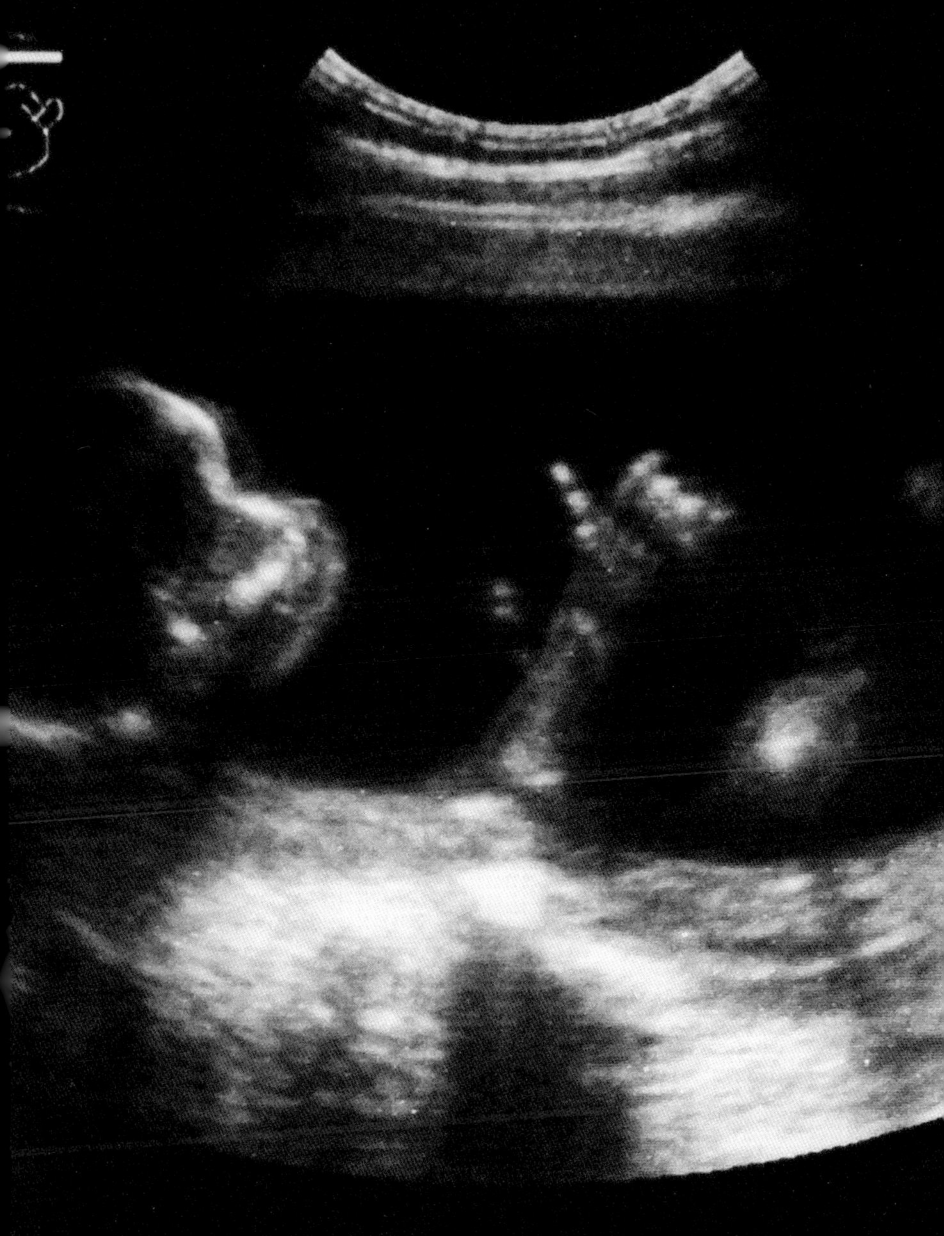

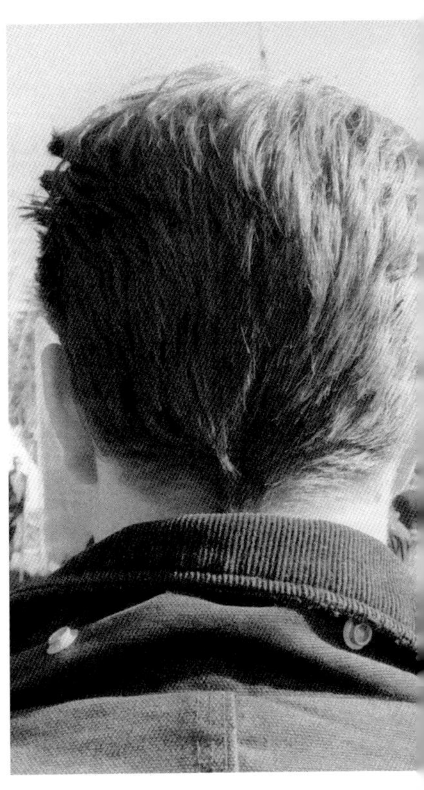

Robert Pattinson,
***The Twilight Saga: Breaking Dawn - Part 2*, 2012**

Raising a child in Hollywood is akin to a Frankenstein experiment. No matter the years of genetic evolution, parental lessons passed down through the few hundred million printed pages of Dr. Spock's books, along with instinctual intellect that lets a mother know when her child needs a warm embrace no matter how far she is from the freshman dorm, nothing could prepare any reproducing being for the environmental influences that Hollywood enacts on its young.

Scan the magazine racks while waiting in line to buy groceries at the store, and you will see stark realities that are the outcomes not necessarily of lousy parenting or botched bloodlines. Instead, you'll see the headlines of quests for acceptance by a host of peers that mimic everything we have all gone through at one point or another, from the halls of high school to the potluck dinners of the suburbs. Instead of jocks and cheerleaders pulling wedgies and toilet-papering pranks on geeks and stoners, Hollywood has critics and journalists, paparazzi and producers, and a whole cast of other make-shift peers waiting to suck the blood and steal the soul of every youth too old to star on the Disney Channel. Although it's not an excuse, there is some understanding of why child actors might gravitate toward a life of addiction and debauchery. Their adolescence is stripped from them by everyone wanting to capitalize on their success, and very few are ever prepared for that. They search out something to numb them from the poking and prodding that everyone is doing to them, and although not literal, the bites and jabs inflict an emotional pain that hazes reality and clouds judgment.

It is often not the parents who are to blame. The culprits tend to be the ones who see monetary value rather than a human being standing in front of a camera. They latch on to the investment because they know that only a few talents in their portfolio will pay off in the long term. The others need to be exploited for as much as they can get before they are cast aside by scandal and public opinion or by a series of movie failures at the box office that are usually out of the control of any actor. And as the stakes increase, so do the attitudes and antics, tantrums thrown for attention, and problems that can't be seen between affairs and afflictions captured in color in this week's tabloids.

Not all Hollywood kids turn out badly. There are a fair share of parenting successes that have yielded the next great directors, writers, producers, and actors. In my field, there is none more evident of this accomplishment of family than that of the Westmores. At face value, the familial nomenclature sounds like an Aaron Spelling drama, generations of doctors or lawyers, staunch and sophisticated, conservative yet highly prominent in all aspects of the city in which they live and control. Except for the career track, the Westmores were all that and more, comprising now four generations of makeup artists that have been instrumental in some of cinema's most memorable moments since 1917. Each generation continues in the family's footsteps as they are the only star on the Walk of Fame dedicated to a family rather

AFTER A FEW MINUTES THAT FELT LIKE FOREVER HOLDING ONTOTHE PHONE, I FINALLY GOT AN ANSWER FROM NANCY'S SECRETARY: "DON'T WORRY, BONNIE, THE SINATRAS ARE TAKING CARE OF YOUR HOSPITAL BILL."

---

than an individual, a triumph in familial values that gives parents hope that they can bestow their lineage with similar success. I have had the pleasure of working with many of the Westmores throughout my career, having been proud to stand with them on a set. Watching them work was always a thrill, knowing the history behind the hands that blushed the faces of Mary Pickford and lined the eyes of Rudolph Valentino. Each one of them was humble, given their stature in the industry. I knew they were an exception to the rule, and since they had a mini monopoly on the beauty business in Hollywood along with Max Factor, I figured my husband and I would try and raise a couple of lawyers or a doctor instead of trying to fill in the gaps between the generations of Westmores.

It was the late 1960s, and I was getting increasingly disappointed when it was my time of the month. My expectations were low when it came to conception. My husband and I weren't giving it the old college try, as we both had our feet on the bottom rung, climbing the career ladder rather than rustling the sheets. I was only twenty-seven, but I should have nearly been a grandmother based on the societal expectations of my Romanian ancestors. My mother gave birth to four children by the time she was forty, and I was tired of answering the question every newlywed hears from everyone: "When are you going to start having babies?" After all, I had walked away from hairstyling glory by refusing to be put in Elvis's studio contract, so I had to make good on my resolve. But, since conceiving a child is all about timing and it seemed we never had enough hours in the day, I would need some divine intervention. Though there would be no star in the east, an old wives' tale involved me kneeling before a queen who would bring my fantasy of motherhood into reality.

Nancy Sinatra and I had a sisterly bond from the moment we met, and that friendship endured decades beyond our production years. While shooting *Speedway*, we often spoke of wanting to have families of our own one day. As we received invitations to baby showers of friends expanding the branches of their family tree, we were left hoping a few seeds might make it our way soon so that we could begin to bloom. As the invitations became more and more lavish, I began to dread the sight of pink and blue in anything that might remind me of what was eluding my loins, at one point wondering if they might have been giving newborns away at Vons Grocery like festive hams during the holidays, as it seemed they were growing like Cabbage Patch Kids. Then, one day, Nancy gave me an invitation with a reassuring pat on the back and a gentle whisper in my ear.

"Don't worry, doll. You'll like this one," she said.

Opening the envelope, I began reading the embossed text, classily center aligned, and upon finishing, my mouth hovered inches from the floor. Nancy stood there, slightly smiling in that snide Sinatra manner. She had learned so well from her father, both of us knowing we had just been invited to the Hollywood version of the nativity.

Emma Roberts, *Grand Champion*, 2002

If it is a little girl's dream to be carried off to a palace by a prince riding a white steed, Priscilla Ann Wagner beat them all by getting scooped up by the King of Rock 'n Roll in a 1967 Cadillac Coup and driven through the gates of Graceland. Years before working with her husband, I remember thinking that it must be just dreamy to be married to Elvis, and when he wed Priscilla, I knew that she must be exceptional. Years later, I learned the truth behind my assumption—not so much about the marriage, but definitely about Priscilla—when we met. More by default than birth, she was worthy of the title of queen regardless of the marriage. She was quiet and polite, dainty in her features but firm in her constitution. Whenever she came onto the set, the tomfoolery that Elvis and the boys were so notable for came to a complete halt, and I immediately knew who cracked the whip in that castle. She always looked as if a court of maidens had coiffed and dressed her, and I always admired her for her ability to smile politely when scores of screaming girls swarmed her and Elvis. The way she said thank you for the compliments they gave her and her husband was sincere, without a single sense of threat to their sanctity.

No matter how much we plan and perceive, we only really know what life has in store once it is handed to us. We primarily never seek out sorrow; pure bliss is always a surprise that is welcomed and savored. Some signs and signals are overlooked, keeping us in suspense until the last moment when our past is put behind us and our future unfurled. The day of Priscilla's baby shower was the epitome of oblivion as to what would change a few hours later, affecting me eternally. I was dressed and ready the morning of the shower before the morning light broke over the crest of the hillside. The anxious adrenaline and anticipating excitement left me with only a few winks of sleep. As I stood in the mirror looking at my polyester mini dress and patent leather boots, I didn't realized that I was looking at myself like this for one of the last times in my life. It was not my outfit or how I styled my hair, but the essence of the interpretation of a woman that a mirror attempts to convey. The reflection of innocence that had become my likeness as a devoted wife was about to open the looking glass into a wonderland that I only now realize so many years later.

I arrived at Nancy's estate with my little gift in hand, a sterling silver porringer and cup, confident the happy couple would understand the thoughtfulness even if it didn't measure up to the expense of the other gifts sitting on the reception table in trademark Tiffany blue boxes. We sat around talking about other peoples' children, the best schools, breastfeeding, and sex because even as ladies, when you get us in a group void of men, that topic always comes up. There were finger foods and champagne, and gifts were opened one at a time, with a chorus of oohs and ahs; the giddiness of the entire afternoon only marred when I was asked by a guest whether my husband and I had children of our own. I was uncomfortable answering that question with anyone, whether they were family or, as proposed now, a friend of a friend. I could never give a straight answer, as I wanted to avoid hearing my voice confirm what sank my heart so profoundly. The tears I was trying to laugh away were suddenly saved from falling from my eyes by a good friend who could tell from across the room that I needed rescuing. Nancy came over and grabbed my hand. Had I known how she was saving me, I would have retreated into a frantic escape from what would happen next.

Tugging me across the room as my heels tried to dig into the shag carpet to impede her persistence, Nancy kept calling out to everyone that it was time for something special. Whatever it was, I realized I was the recipient of

Sc 268 D42

2/29

EXT. Denali: House

ALASKA

Kristen Stewart, *The Twilight Saga: Breaking Dawn - Part 2*, 2012

that "something special." As I was being pulled closer and closer to Priscilla, whatever the plan involved, I grew more and more fearful of what Nancy had up her sleeve. Nancy had yanked me to a stop in front of Priscilla, my brow arching with shock and confusion. Looking at Priscilla, beaming with her warm smile and soft eyes, I sighed with relief, hoping it would all be over soon. Nancy began boasting about an old Italian wives' tale, my face beet red with her proclamation that my husband and I were having trouble conceiving. She went on to explain that rubbing the stomach of a woman who was about to give birth would give luck to another woman, basically guaranteeing conception. I was hoping that it was only a story being told, but when Nancy forcefully placed my hands on Priscilla's perfect bulge, on the verge of bursting, the blood rushed out of my shoulders down to my hands. The tingle in my fingertips made it impossible to lift my arms. Priscilla moved my wrists in circles on her stomach, and with one kick from the baby inside, my hands came alive, the movement of my hands larger and faster, thinking that if I did it enough, this might work. Priscilla winked at me as I withdrew my hands, and the room filled with applause and congratulations. Nancy stood there, arms folded, a Cheshire Cat of a grin filled her face with a smooth confidence that a venerable myth from Sicily had transcended time and proved itself again, right there in Hollywood.

A few weeks later, Nancy and I were on the road in Northern California, and my husband came up for the weekend to visit. Suppose you have ever been to Big Sur. In that case, you will know that it does not take any more than the sound of the surf battering the rocks close to a cottage tucked in between the redwood trees, along with a bottle of wine from a vineyard nearby, to spark a little romance and then some between a young married couple that has been apart for more than a few days. Six weeks later, I returned to Nancy's house unannounced, carrying a basket of daisies, her favorite flower. I walked around the back of the house to the kitchen where she was, and when she opened the door to greet me, she had that same wide, wry smile as she did after her folly that day with Priscilla and me.

"You're pregnant!" she exclaimed as if she'd known it all along without a fraction of a doubt.

She hugged me tightly, ushered me in, and we spent a good portion of the afternoon sipping tea and talking about the doctor, how I was feeling, and sex because that's what two ladies talk about when they are left alone in the afternoon without a man in the room.

Nancy Sinatra touched my life in ways I would never believe, not just once but again when she followed up with an encore about nine months later. I had been put on the Sinatra family payroll with a retainer for my services in case anyone should need them. This helped a lot with all the bills associated with pregnancy, and in those days, the currency exchange made them similar to the mound of expenses that exist today. To make ends meet, I worked at MGM into my third trimester, even running into Elvis one day, who hadn't seen me since *Speedway* and proclaimed, "Looks like you had an accident," followed by a big hug, and listening intently to the story of Nancy's antics nine months ago. I had been home in bed for several weeks when, one night, I got up to go to the bathroom, and the leaky shower wasn't the only thing that had its water broken. My husband packed my small suitcase and helped me waddle to the front door before disappearing back inside to vomit one more time from the nervousness he tried to hide for his virile masculinity. We drove to the hospital in Glendale,

Natalie Portman, *Anywhere But Here*, 1998

Keanu Reeves, *Tune in Tomorrow*, 1990

and they checked me in as the labor pains began to swell significantly through the night into the early morning hours. We were both nervous with all the questions first parents typically had in their minds, but when he returned from speaking with the doctor, I knew something was not right about their discussion. He told me that, most likely, I would have to have a Caesarean section and that our insurance did not cover that procedure. As the baby pushed, I felt the wind knocked out of my lungs, making it impossible to speak. I pointed to my purse so my husband could get my address book.

As he flipped through the pages, I suddenly held my hand out, pressed my finger against a name, took one deep breath, and managed to eke out, "Remind me to call that number when this is over."

As the nurses scurried me out the door, I tried to remember any technique I had learned in our natural childbirth classes, already forgetting the name I had indicated under the "S" tab of my contacts.

A short time later, I gave birth to our son, Jason, whose name we had chosen when Barbara Streisand told me what she named her son while working on *Hello, Dolly!* The following week, my husband reminded me to make the call that I couldn't recall asking him to remember through the waves of contractions and blurred vision of birthing. Yet, when he showed me the phone number for Boots Entertainment, I knew exactly why I needed to call Nancy Sinatra at her production company. Having worked on *Movin'* with Nancy and the rest of the Sinatra family, I had been told I may be eligible to participate in their company health insurance plan.

After a few minutes that felt like forever holding onto the phone, I finally got an answer from Nancy's secretary: "Don't worry, Bonnie, the Sinatras are taking care of your hospital bill."

With a huge sigh of relief and my son cuddled up on my bare chest, I would forever be thankful for the kindness the Sinatra family extended to my family that day.

Our daughter, Dana, didn't require any voodoo or witchcraft to bring about. After accomplishing it once before, having a different mindset and much trying, along with a few tricks in the delivery room, was all it took to deliver her into our family. The discussions began about whether we should raise our children in Los Angeles. While we hadn't personally known anyone who had encountered significant problems with raising their kids, there were plenty of indications of the effects of Hollywood on others that appeared each week in the news. My husband and I did not doubt our abilities as parents, but it was the same mentality that applied to driving a car. It's not your skill that you're worried about. It's that of the other drivers on the road. As has been confirmed for centuries, and still holds to the fact today, we can do everything in our power as parents to protect our children from the influence of others, just short of locking them in a cupboard under the stairs. But, at some point, you have to hope and pray that all the lessons you have instilled in them will resonate when the situation arises and that your child will think before they follow someone jumping from the proverbial bridge. The one element we could change would be to put them in an environment where the temptations and tribulations would be minimized. If the moon was the safest, Hollywood was the furthest away from that expectation. With good jobs, a comfortable home, and the right ideals instilled from our lineage, we needed a sign from the unknown to convince us to shake it all up. And that is precisely what we received one February morning.

There is no way to explain the feeling of an earthquake until you have been in one, but when you live in Southern California, the next thing on your mind after you run to get into a doorway is how long it will last. The San Fernando Quake of 1971 seemed as if it would never end. My husband and I had a plan for protecting the children in the event of a quake, and like many instincts associated with parenthood, there was no thought or review of procedures; we just sprang into action. Our daughter was in a crib in our room, and I pulled her into my arms as my husband struggled to get down the hall, bouncing back and forth between the walls and into our son's room. After it seemed as if the earth would open wide and swallow us whole, the shattering of dishes that had been a sonic sled of sound became an occasional crash of glass, the anticipation of the finality of the event much like the last kernels of corn popping in their microwave-safe bag. After assessing the physical condition of our family, we were fine, besides having two terrified infants screaming in the silence that moments before had been a symphony of earthen growls.

We stepped over fallen furniture and books strewn across the floor and through the kitchen, careful of the contents of the cupboards that had emptied onto the tile, only discernible as a set of dishes by the teacup handles. Exiting the back door, we gathered on the driveway and stared at the sky turning pale blue in the first hour of daylight. With my husband's arm around me, my daughter clutched closely as our son wrapped himself around his father's leg; sturdy to the ground, we realized that our sign hadn't come from the heavens but from deep below us, and our decision for how we would raise our children had been made.

The earthquake wasn't the only reason we left our home on the West Coast for Indiana. Still, the fear in our children's eyes that morning, along with financial and family prospects, was a culmination of reasons enough to pack the car and head back east across the northern states. Our family had grown outside of our small tribe, and most of them had children the ages of ours and had settled within a few hours of each other in the Midwest. While I peered over the seat and through the rear window, watching one of my dreams disappear further away with each mile marker of Interstate 10, what I assumed was even more apparent. Once you become a parent, life is all about someone else before yourself. The years we spent in Indianapolis and the surrounding area were some of the fondest memories of family and the kids we have. While we didn't avoid all the problems associated with integrating our children with others, it was still our best decision. Although we had made the right move, I still found myself watching television and going to movies and sitting there, immovable, during the credits, looking for the names of people I had worked with, and feeling a little empty when someone else's filled the space next to "hairstylist" where mine had once been. I believed life was full of signs, and my well of hopes had not dried up, although what brought me back to the film business was the most challenging path of the journey we could have ever taken.

While I stayed home and raised the children, working briefly in a hair salon at a department store, my husband grew in his career and eventually started his own business. While he was as bright as it gets, nothing could stave off a lull in the industry. After building our first home and moving into an even nicer house across from a small lake, we sat the children, now nearing their double-digit years, outside in the backyard one Saturday and tried to explain to them what bankruptcy meant as they equated our loss of everything in terms of friends and classmates that were priceless beyond our debt. I remembered my husband and I turning the key in the lock on the door the last time, the car packed once again for the move back west. Our eyes filled with tears at losing what we had tried so hard to keep, but our solace was in our minds, and we were filled now with making everything right again for all of us. For me, we were heading in the right direction of my dream as a hairstylist; the only problem is that we would only get some of the way there. Instead of heading straight west, we took a southern route to a place we only knew from watching a television series on Friday nights about a family with a guy named J.R. and the city they lived in. Even though my husband had a good job offer, the shiny buildings gleaming on the screen reminded me of Oz and the promise that better times for all of us were through the tumbleweed to a place called Dallas.

In the early '80s, Dallas, Texas, was a burgeoning metropolis of cultural influences beyond its moniker of oil wells and rodeos. Opportunities were everywhere, and the arts started making their marks on gallery walls, radio airwaves, and big and small screens in homes and malls. When we turned off the highway, I knew we were about a thousand miles short of Hollywood, but little did I know that our detour in life was a shortcut right back into the business. Not only was the television show of the same name filmed around the city, but the studios at Las Colinas had been built, and productions from California were now being shot in Texas at locations around the state. I had yet to realize that this was becoming common with filming. Years ago, it was quite rare for a film or television show to be shot on location outside of the studio lots or surrounding area since the landscape of Southern California can easily be transformed into the desert of Cleopatra. Main Street USA still sits on the back lot of Warner Bros. All the time had passed, and through it all, I kept my dream alive, waiting patiently for a blessing in disguise. When I received the call to work on my first production a few miles from our home in Plano, I realized that my persistence in parenting had been rewarded personally. Showing up on the set, the first day was filled with a new set of jitters and fears, but after giving birth to two children and enduring the disappointments of declaring bankruptcy, there wasn't anything that I wasn't capable of on or off a movie set.

As I began doing more and more films and series, the requests to travel to Los Angeles became increasingly frequent, and I knew one day we would return to Hollywood. The lessons we learned as parents, handed down now to our teenage children, were all we could do, and when we did return to Southern California, our departure had come full circle for us. We had to make that journey with our young family to feel the reward of returning to fulfill our adult dreams. While I knew that our kids entering their second decade still had a lot to learn and avoid, I felt pretty confident that whatever difficulties they faced or mistakes they made, there was a good chance I wouldn't find out about it from reading *The Inquirer.*

AFTER ALL, I DIDN'T NEED A NEWS RAG TO TELL ME IF MY CHILD WAS IN TROUBLE OR NEEDED ME. I'M A MOTHER, AND MY INSTINCTS WOULD ALREADY KNOW.

Hilary Swank, *The Reaping*, 2007

7-22-99 / 7-23-99

Sc. 24, 25 D4
M&U's office

BISCUITS & GRAVY

In this day and age, we are all looking for a bit of simplicity in our lives. But, in searching for simplicity in our relationships, jobs, holidays, and the ability to remember the little things, life has become a more complex task than it was for any of our forefathers. The gadgets and gizmos that permeate every moment of our existence, while we are conscious and wandering through our days or fast asleep floating through our dreams, have replaced mundane with maniacal. For an eighty-three-year-old woman, it requires a mental wheelchair to traverse across the house, not to set off an alarm or bring the entire Internet to a halt with the wrong push of a button on the television remote.

We all thought our parents had it difficult. Without automated systems and technological advancements, the fact that merely talking to another human being was able to get us to the twenty-first century is still a mystery to the Xbox generation. I remember watching my father leave the house at four in the morning every day. He would trudge through the snow to his old milk truck to deliver glass bottles door to door. After delivering the milk, he would gently pick up the empty bottles placed on each doorstep and take them back to the bottling plant to get washed and refilled. While familiar, this seemed a laborious task that was a large production for something as simple as milk. Yet there were thousands, and millions, of these tasks that happened every day. Mail was sorted by hand, telephone operators had to be contacted to connect a call to the neighbors next door, and paper carriers rode bicycles with rolls of newsprint that they had rubber banded themselves, throwing with the accuracy of an NFL quarterback. At the same time, they pedaled rapidly to increase their chances of receiving a nickel tip when they came to collect payment for their services at the end of the month.

Our search for simplicity has exponentially made our lives more difficult. As you can imagine, there is absolutely nothing simple about Hollywood, from the people to the highways; for example, avoiding oncoming traffic while making a left turn on Wilshire Boulevard with a camera waiting to snap a mug shot of your hatchback hybrid and send it to your email address. At the pinnacle of it all, the movie-making process in the culmination of everything the search for simplicity has failed to achieve.

Like most of us, I remember the first movie I ever saw. At the Paramount Theater in Aurora, Illinois, I sat watching *House of Wax*. The ornate ceiling and the oversized, cushioned seats that had comforted me as the red velvet drapes parted and the lights dimmed now hovered over me in horror as my screams surpassed those of Phyllis Kirk as she tried to escape Vincent Price lingering at every corner. With each of my worst fears projected bigger than life in front of my very eyes, the fingers on my left hand became more impervious to the ice-cold soda as my right crushed a box of my favorite candy, Good 'N Plenty. My feet swung back and forth restlessly, a groundless sprint, until the symphonic soundtrack subsided with another slender escape from the hall of mirrors, my heart rate returning to

George Clooney, *Ocean's Eleven*, 2001

a normal pace and lips widely smiling with the recess of adrenaline, my mouth a cornucopia of concession stand flavors. Sitting in the darkened, crowded theater, I looked around at the dimly lit faces of those around me, staring in their own ways at the shimmering screen. Some were quizzical, others confused; the lady next to me had nearly chewed her monogrammed handkerchief to shreds while a man in the row behind me slept, grumbling softly as he watched an entirely different series of events unfold in his slumber. I realized in that matinee that everyone seated there was experiencing something different; even though the same actors spoke the same lines, each person was affected differently. Movies have had that effect throughout history, rallying citizens behind wars, defining political movements, empowering the impoverished, and aiding the baby boomers in leaving their mark on the planet's population through romantic comedies shown at drive-ins, watched in bits and pieces from the backseat of a '57 Chevy.

This power of movies to elicit emotions and raise awareness was a concept I grasped early on in life, and only now do I realize what an impact I have been able to have with the work I have done, along with the countless other crew members of movies we have made together. Choosing to make a particular film is an absolute responsibility and liability. And with this ability to rattle emotions and alter perceptions, simplicity is often the best recipe for success in Hollywood and life. In life, as in a screenplay, the more complicated things are, the greater the chance of failure.

The first set I ever walked onto was the TV series *Green Acres* back in 1965. The General Services Studios on Las Palmas Drive wasn't the biggest of production lots or the fanciest, but it was my first. As usual, the first of something in life seemed like nothing could be better, and I always remembered it as my first studio experience. I went to the hair and makeup room and unpacked my styling kit, which consisted of various sized hair irons, a small hair iron heater stove, bobby pins, a brush, and a comb. The meticulous rearranging of my styling tools was a front for the nervousness that had me digging my heels into the wood floor. Then Eva Gabor walked into the room and sat down in a chair. For the next hour, I must have silently said the Rosary a hundred times, and somehow, through a blur of combing and ironing, I molded her blonde locks into a mountain of a beehive ready for the camera. Eva confidently rose, took one last look in the mirror, and walked to set as I gathered a brush, hairspray bottle, and a few more bobby pins on my way out the door.

Stepping onto the set was similar to walking through the rainforest without a machete. There was a madness to the order of setting up for the first shot of the day, and it was not all that far away from a pack of primates just released from captivity. People ran around jumping over Styrofoam boulders and climbing ladders that disappeared into the darkness beyond, where others were frantically running across catwalks swaying from chains attached to the ceiling. Cables uncoiled and slithered, dull black endless serpents, around a makeshift train depot and off through a small gathering of Papier-mâché oak trees on the far side of the stage. Enormous lights perched atop shiny silver stands, a forest of metal, electricity, and illumination that required an adventure guide to navigate safely to my destination, a tall set chair with my actress' name in bold white letters on the backrest. And there I stood alone, with heavy and immovable feet, terrified to take my first step into the wilds of Hollywood.

Trying not to faint on my first day, motionless, I held

my eyes shut for a few seconds and took in the sounds around me. Set builders were hammering like the men who had repaired my parent's grocery store after a fire when I was a child. People's voices were a memory of shouting at the butcher counter, trying to buy a roast the night before Christmas. Footsteps shuffling and stopping hurriedly reminded me of a Sears and Roebuck, knowing where to find the latest fashion but stopping to look in the mirror and check a lip line before reaching the dressing room. This environment was both prehistoric and futuristic to the eyes, but to the senses, it was familiar, filled with recollections of people and places I had seen and survived before. My breathing became even, and I slowly opened my eyes, taking in my surroundings, which weren't so scary anymore. My hands no longer shook, and my feet were solid and sturdy. I walked through the maze of light stands and electrical wires, put down my bag, and began to make the final touches to Eva's hairstyle.

A few minutes later, I cleared my voice with a few precise pushes of hairpins in the right location and confidently said, "Ms. Gabor, you're ready for set."

Since that day, I have seen a few things change in this world. Dick Tracy wristwatches and Buck Rogers's computers didn't even come close to the personal computer and a little something most of us carry around in our pockets in the form of a smartphone. I still send out holiday greeting cards with postage stamps, but I mail and pay bills electronically every other day of the year. Grocery delivery is still around, but it is most efficient when using a mobile application that doesn't even require a voice conversation with someone or the exchange of physical currency. When we bought our first television in the '60s, it was black and white and required a little extra tin foil on

IT ALWAYS HELPS TO HAVE FRIENDS IN LIFE AND IN TINSEL TOWN. THEY ARE DIFFICULT T O FIND AND TOUGHER TO KEEP HOLD OF, BUT WHEN YOU FIND A TRUE FRIEND, THEY ARE THERE TO PICK YOU UP AND MOVE YOU FORWARD WITH THE UTMOST CARING AND CONCERN.

---

the antenna to get six channels, although seven were listed in the TV Guide. Now, I can watch almost every television show by simply tapping a button on a digital tablet and wirelessly projecting it onto a fifty-inch flat screen with ten million colors and a feature called surround sound, which resembles the sound system at the nearby multiplex theater. Trying to keep up with the changes in this world in the past decade has me warding off the latest and greatest while constantly searching for ways to preserve traditions from the past.

The basic craft of moviemaking has stayed the same since the day it began. Someone comes up with a story, and many people with particular skills use tools to capture the story visually. Then, all the pieces of the film get put together, someone writes a few songs, it gets shown on a screen, and people either love it or could care less. The difference now is that the simplicity of movie making has been complicated through time and invention, by both business and innovation. Back in the day, when a studio wanted to make a movie, they typed out a budget, and we all went to work with the hopes and aspirations that whatever movie or television show we were making would be well received by the audience and, hopefully, cover the costs. The film business has over-complicated itself with fear

MIAMI
SHARKS

Dennis Quaid, Al Pacino, *Any Given Sunday*, 1999

of failure, opting to over-analyze risk above creativity. Multi-institutional financing is required after data assessing the popularity ratings of talent and crew. The cost of advertising is offset with consumer promotional agreements such as merchandise and product placement, as if a toy in a fast-food meal will sway a child's opinion of an animated movie. While the glaring eyes of journalistic scrutiny and social influencers seek shock factor merely for likes in chat threads, it thwarts the efforts of so many people who want to make a great movie.

Then, there is technology and innovation that puts the virtual wrench on the whole process. The simplicity of that first set and most of the films I worked on in my first two decades make it seem like we were inventing the wheel and fire when compared with working on *Snow White and the Huntsman* in London in the Fall of 2011. I have seen crews grow from double digits to low triples, working from three weeks to a few months. Still, when it takes fifteen hundred people, three camera crews, and at least six months to make a film, the word "simple" might as well be an expletive; you wouldn't dare mention it if your mother was nearby and you had a head start down the hallway. Painted backdrops depicting the countryside in the Midwest have been replaced by vibrant blue and green screens that will eventually depict snow-laden haunted forests that reach the horizon filled with ominous clouds that an artist rendered on a computer. I thought putting a camera on a crane was ingenious until I saw remote-controlled helicopters and zip lines with cameras racing through the air. We still shoot on film sometimes. Still, that process is becoming less frequent as digitally capturing three thousand hours of filming makes it more efficient and much less costly. Thank goodness my blow dryers and curling irons only have one button, and a comb is still a comb.

It isn't as if the entire filmmaking community denies that getting a movie from concept to production and post-production to theaters is complex. But we all look for simplicity in our jobs, and finding those simple details keeps the complexity manageable. That doesn't just hold true for Hollywood; it reaches beyond the Grand Canyon, over the golden plains, and into suburbs and small towns worldwide. Juggling a family, a marriage, a bossy boss, and a relationship on the rocks can be a solitary circus performance worth the Ringling Brothers's title. We all have our own complexities in life. How we balance them with simplicity gives each of us peace of mind.

On more than one occasion while filming, I tried to find simplicity for myself, and it ended up being the common denominator in a group of us throughout the production and beyond. Sometimes, simplicity is searching for antiques in farm towns outside Pittsburgh; other times, it is sightseeing villages in the Welsh countryside. Still, simplicity is often a home-cooked meal shared with friends who have bonded on set, searching for comfort after a brutal week of filming. There's only one rule in cooking comfort food: if it becomes too complex, there is nothing comfortable about it, and unfortunately, that pertains to chateaubriand and chocolate soufflé. Tim Allen holds the award in my heart for being a comfort food connoisseur. After sitting there day after day for hours, getting into his *The Santa Clause 2* makeup and hair, he just wanted a little slice of Detroit, which he indeed called home. I asked him what his favorite sandwich was, as working with a fork and knife was nearly impossible with his prosthetic fat fingers.

"Spam on toasted Wonder Bread."

Having been a fan of canned mystery meat manufactured and processed in Minnesota, USA, I made Tim's wish come true a few months later as the stewardess on the private plane we were flying in brought out an assortment of snacks along with the sliced Spam that I had snuck onto the flight. On that multi-million-dollar jet, the most priceless thing on board was Tim's laughter, so jolly it would have made even Ole Saint Nick envious.

Although Spam only brought true joy to one man on that set, one of my favorite comfort foods and the simplest recipe I have ever created brought joy to one of the most prestigious casts ever assembled for a blockbuster movie. Having been a fan of many originals, it was a thrill to be asked to be a part of the 2001 remake of *Ocean's Eleven*. I had worked on four previous films that Steven Soderbergh directed, but this was by far his most significant production, with a cast that any director would dream of orchestrating. There is no need to list the names as they are as recognizable as George, Brad, Matt, and Julia. When they came together for three months in the Nevada desert, the heat they created together onscreen was hotter than any table game in the casino. And with all of them staying in the same hotel, the attention they drew from adoring fans and paparazzi made it challenging to wander outside without a mass of security.

We found ourselves most nights in secluded gaming rooms or villas, laughing and telling stories while sharing a few cocktails, or better yet, playing practical jokes on each other, a time-honored tradition in Hollywood that I had shared since the beginning days and still through today. Clooney had his toilet seat shrouded with Saran Wrap, Damon was short-sheeted, and my son and I would roll all the large planters from the hallway in front of Roberts's door so she would have to call maintenance to move them

Hilary Swank, *P.S. I Love You*, 2007

IN OUR SEARCH FOR SIMPLICITY, WE HAVE EXPONENTIALLY MADE OUR LIVES MORE DIFFICULT, DRAINED OUR MEMORY CAPACITY, AND CREATED ENOUGH SPACE BETWEEN A FAMILY OF FOUR EATING DINNER AT APPLEBEE'S THAT YOU WOULD THINK THEY WERE SITTING AT ONE OF HENRY THE VIII'S TABLES RATHER THAN A CORNER BOOTH NEAR THE SALAD BAR.

---

to make her call time.

After a month or so, whether staying at a five-star resort or being catered for by an award-winning chef such as Wolfgang Puck, the food, without offense to anyone, gets a little monotonous, and homesickness sets in. Nothing beats homemade comfort food to help stave off the production blues. While I was staying in a common room in the hotel, Julia and the rest of the headliners stayed in the expansive bungalows with multiple bedrooms and private swimming pools, but more importantly, full kitchens, which most didn't use. Still, I made good use of them on more than one occasion. And when I fired up the oven and turned on the stove, the smell of home cooking was the culinary equivalent of the Pied Piper. The front doorbell kept ringing like eager children getting a whiff of dinner after the last snowball was thrown at the opposing forces; they cast off their shoes and rushed to the dining room table, waiting to be fed the sustenance that would warm their bellies, refuel their hearts, and rejuvenate their souls. The difference was that these were Oscar winners and former *People* magazine "Sexist Man Alive" recipients who chose to eat something even Oprah Winfrey didn't believe they would consume.

I have been famous for a few things, like nearly gluing Elvis's hands together. Still, I am legendary in Hollywood for being able to cook the best biscuits and gravy that anyone has ever had, at least according to Julia Roberts, who told that to a few million people when asked by an astonished Oprah on one of her shows. It's not anything secret, and it's something I am eager to reveal. Milk, some flour, a generous amount of black pepper, one pack of regular and one pack of spicy sausage, and canned biscuits to add a little crunch.

Bonnie Cheveving

Biscuits & Gravy

1 lb. Hot Pork Sausage
1 lb. Regular Pork Sausage
fry together and Chop up into
Chunks but not to Fine

1/4 cup Flour & 3 cups Milk
wisk Flour & 1 cup Milk First to Dissolve Flour
Then add rest of Milk to sausage

Biscuits
Use any box biscuit mix or refrigerated
biscuits, Bake as directed.

Pour Sausage Gravy over individual biscuits.
Add Fresh ground pepper or Chili Flakes on top

While often there have been attempts to repeat the recipe, I've been told the taste isn't the same, and I know precisely the reason. When filming amidst the complexity of a major motion picture, sequestered away from the public and the comforts of home, the simplest reminder of everyday life—away from the lights, cameras, and over-oxygenated hotel rooms—is something as simple as sausage, biscuits, and gravy that helps us endure. It is a reminder that there is something beyond the glitz and glamour, the adoration and obsession, the fame and fortune. In the end, moviemaking is still as simple as a bunch of talented people who, while slightly extraordinary, still have the same eyes, ears, hands, and feet as almost everyone else. We all desire simplicity in a business that has become complex. While we feel nostalgic for the past's simplicity, the intricacy of the future is truly awe-inspiring.

Each time I put the key in the front door of my home after returning from a grueling production that has taken me far away for months at a time, my first order of business beyond the stack of mail and magazines is to fill the refrigerator and cupboard with everything that was missing from a late-night room service menu. While I haven't figured out the app on my mobile, I still go to the grocery store and let the clerk scan my items for fear of shutting down the entire store if I try the self-checkout method. I come home and cook myself something simple, give a little taste to my hairless Chinese crested, Weezle, while sitting on the sofa, trying to turn on the TV with a remote that mimics NASA's Mission Control. Finally hitting the correct series of buttons, the TV illuminates, and I pull my feet off the floor and take a few bites of a cookie I've been craving, refueling my heart and soul. With a sly grin, I think of all those actors attempting to make biscuits and gravy the next morning in their own homes, the quizzical look on their faces as they wonder why it just doesn't taste the same.

I LET OUT A GIRLISH GIGGLE AS WEEZLE SLIDES UNDER THE BLANKET TO WARM MY TOES.

05

CHARACTER

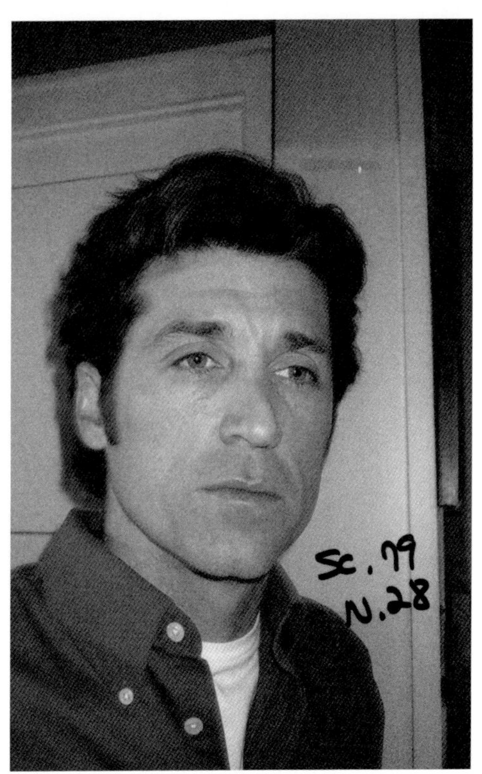

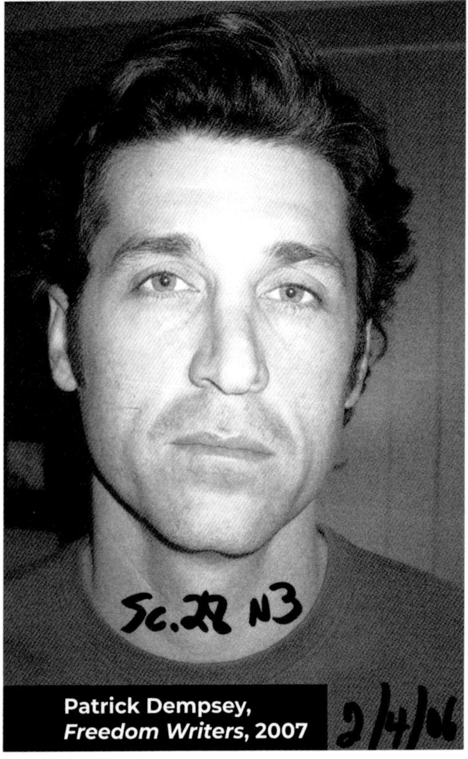

Patrick Dempsey,
***Freedom Writers*, 2007**

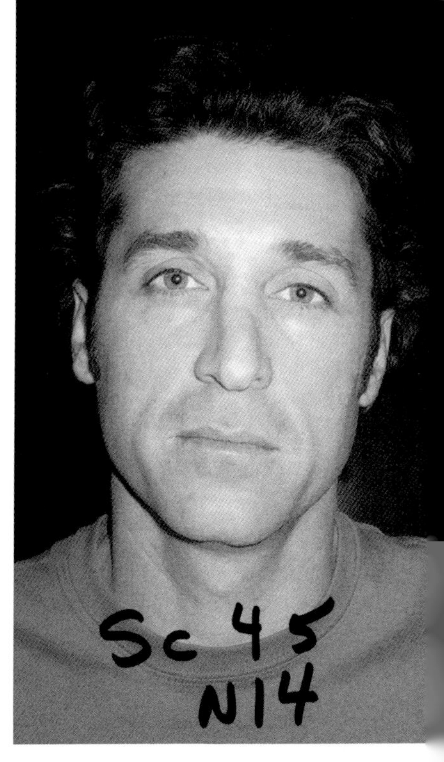

The essence of moviemaking is suspension of disbelief. I've been five feet away from that statement with an "I wouldn't believe it if I hadn't seen it myself" more than a hundred times.

After all, I've worked with the half-dead, contributed to the robbery of a Vegas casino, and touched up Santa Claus's flowing white hair right before he went off to fly on a reindeer. When I told friends and family what I had been working on before it was released in the theater, they probably wondered if I had finally fallen off my rocker.

When they first called me to work on The Twilight Saga films, I read the first script and said, "They think somebody is going to buy a ticket to this teen vampire movie?"

A billion-plus dollars and a few franchise films later, I realized that sanity and insanity are figures of speech and not applicable to the film business.

Growing up in Illinois, I remember going to the theater to watch the matinee on Saturday. My tiny jaw was agape with what I saw projected in front of my eyes, completely oblivious that I would be on the other side of that screen

Phil Hartman, *Sgt. Bilko*, 1996

HOWEVER, AS IS THE CASE FOR MOST OF LIFE, PERCEPTION HAS EVERYTHING TO DO WITH WHAT ONE PERSON CALLS CRAZY AND WHAT ANOTHER EMBRACES. WEIRD IS LOVELY TO SOME AND JUST PLAIN ODD TO OTHERS. BUT ANYTIME I'VE LOOKED AT SOMETHING AND THOUGHT, "THAT'S TOO WEIRD," I TAKE A SECOND LOOK AND TRY TO UNDERSTAND THE PERSON BEYOND THE INITIAL PERCEPTION.

---

one day. A humble upbringing left little time to dream, and hope was something that cost money, of which we had very little. I started working in what people would now define as child labor, tried to be a good student, and grew up wanting a life that landed somewhere between conventional and ordinary. In my early twenties, I would have settled for a sliver of the American Dream and eaten that humble pie for the rest of my life.

Sometime after my husband and I moved to Los Angeles, I started to get crazy ideas in my head. Blame it on the smog, glittering boulevard, or something swirling in the breeze from that stuff hippies were smoking outside The Whisky a Go Go. I started to succumb to lunacy over the idea that I wanted to join the circus. Not the one with an oversized top and sword swallower, but the movie business, which has all the same thrills but a few more side shows than Barnum and Bailey's. Although my husband was always supportive of my endeavor into the lunacy, I am sure there were a few conversations behind my back between my sisters that suggested a road trip to California to rescue me from my madness. The excitement of seeing something impossible become possible every day on set was intoxicating. In the beginning, mainly, but throughout my career, I cherished the journey of developing my craft that I didn't know I had inside me.

Even though I grew up in a place of nothing theatrical, the most creative person around me was the boy wearing the high school mascot costume; there was this ability to visualize the unseen and unleash it into reality. I have climbed through every branch of my family tree to find anything etched in the bark that would suggest a single creative gene I possess. The only thing that comes to mind is the graffiti my brother sprayed on the side of abandoned buildings near the Fox River, which I considered art at that young age. While people can study to become creative, there was something ingrained inside of me that I translated into creative art through a lot of hard work, failure, and finally, just figuring it out. We are all a bit nuts because the artist knows how to make something out of it, and the layman fights to keep it from coming out at all the wrong times. Once the artist is unleashed, it's an addiction without a cure and something I have craved from my first taste of the creative Kool-Aid.

When my husband and I moved the kids to Indiana in the early 1970s, I realized how much I craved creativity. I took a job in the salon at L.S. Ayres, but the Midwest simplicity kept my creative juices far from flowing. In an attempt to lull my craving, I entered cooking competitions. Once, to my amazement, I won the best salad category for some concoction that I perfected, to the distaste of my family, who ate it for dinner far too many times. Macramé, disco dancing lessons, and finishing anything my daughter did for a badge in Girl Scouts were never near enough to compare to what I had experienced in those early years of my career in Hollywood. I yearned for the mayhem of movie making, the quest to make the impossible possible, and being part of a community that embraced the weird and wonderful. So, when the family moved to Texas in the early '80s, I could finally quench that thirst for creativity with movies of the week and a little-known TV series called *Dallas*.

However, as is the case for most of life, perception has everything to do with what one person calls crazy and what another embraces. Weird is lovely to some and just plain odd to others. But anytime I've looked at something and thought, "That's too weird," I take a second look and try to understand the person beyond the initial perception. Usually, I'm pleasantly surprised at how a second look opens my eyes to the wonderfulness of weirdness.

Working at the studios in the 1960s was a daily dose of the perception of character. I remember the first day I experienced Doris Day stride into the makeup room clutching nearly a dozen leashes which, on the other ends of which, adorned in bedazzled collars, pranced six standard poodles with blue, green, and pink dyed fur. If you did not know that was Doris, you might think that woman was way off the deep end. However, understanding Ms. Day's character, anyone would be sincerely sympathetic to realize that she was not only a commercial supporter of rescue shelters, but that the dogs gave her comfort as she suffered from severe anxiety. Her little tufted troop of canines was her constant hug of comfort, distraction from depression, and confidence to step in front of the camera so that she could help us all forget about our trials and tribulations with the comedic moments she gave us.

When I recollect the massive number of characters I helped create for all those movies, I often drew on the

Jodie Foster, *Little Man Tate*, 1991

Cameron Diaz, *Any Given Sunday*, 1999

Keanu Reeves, *Tune in Tomorrow*, 1990

characters of people that I crossed paths with during my lifetime. Whenever I would receive a script for a film I was about to work on, I would go through a process called "breaking down the script." Generally, this process consisted of reading the script three times and focusing on the story, character, and craft. I will skip explaining the story read for the obvious and jump to the craft read. This was where I looked at technical aspects of production that may have required additional hair assistants for large crowd scenes, special effects such as natural or computer-generated effects, and complex hairstyles that required additional prep and application time. All too often in many of the films I worked on, the demands on an actor's hair were going to be physically severe, or length and texture were different from their natural hair type, so a wig needed to be made weeks ahead of time so that it fit perfectly and was the correct color. These visual choices would then be outlined in a continuity breakdown, so I knew which styles, applications, and hair pieces would be used for multiple scenes or may require repair because of a stunt or a scene with artificial rain.

With the character read, I pulled from not only the literal description in the text but also images and historical references, such as the silly 'ratty' wig for Joe Pesci when he played David Ferry in *JFK*. Many people saw that film and thought, "What a horrible wig. Who was the miserable hairstylist for that film?" Not every film I did involved making someone glamorous. Still, that character represented the natural person often teased about his hair behind his back. So, my answer to the critics is, "I nailed that look." Other hair designs were a product of what the fictional character would have weighted the importance of her "looks" to the character in terms of career, environment, or circumstance. For instance, Hilary Swank's character, Katherine, in *The Reaping*, is a former missionary who travels to a small town to investigate biblical plagues that seem to be occurring. The location of that town in the film was in and around Baton Rouge, Louisiana. That character would only be concerned with looking well-put-together at some hours of the day. She is trudging through swamps, battling locusts, and trying not to be carted off to the afterlife by Satan. The climate is hot and humid, situations uncomfortable, and everything adrenaline-charged almost every moment, so the character would try to be somewhat kempt, mostly staying relaxed and comfortable and not having to deal with hair in her face. Hilary and I decided she would wear her hair back, either with a clip or a tie, and it was the most accurate representation of the character, giving her the confidence to portray the role in its best light and ultimately save everyone from the apocalypse.

The decisions of the film's characters and actors are also partly based on reality. There is a need for an actor to connect with the character on some personal level or lack thereof to convey authenticity to an audience. This is also important for me when developing the look for a single actor or the overall theme for an entire cast when I am the department head. Films like *Mona Lisa Smile* are more constrained in the overall look because they are period pieces based in a specific location, such as a conservative private girls' school and a particular decade like the 1950s. However, even though location and time may dictate an overall theme to the hair design, it is my job to manipulate that theme by choosing when to allow the hairstyle to illustrate the character's subconscious. For instance, Julia Roberts plays a free-thinking art professor who enlightens Kirsten Dunst, Julia Stiles, and Maggie Gyllenhaal to different views on social norms. When Julia and the girls are publicly in a school setting, they wear their hair coifed, pulled back, and styled. However, in private, individually or together, they

Julia Roberts, Los Angeles, California, 2005

Hugh Grant, *Nine Months*, 1995

wear their hair down, free from the confines of hairpins and ponytails. This is so that an audience sees them as rebellious and without the restraints of the perception of behavioral expectations of women during that period. Subtle changes to the hair define the characters and the character traits at different times to propel the story and give more dimension to the narrative participants.

Character perception is essential when defining two characters to create tension and conflict. One of the main narrative forces that keeps an audience on the edge of their seat is a character's ability to go against the norm, make choices that do not agree with others, and find pathways to an uncharted or borderline reckless solution. One of the most challenging sets of characters I developed the looks for were actually played by the same actor, making all my choices even more difficult and critical. Edward Norton played Bill and Brady Kincaid in *Leaves of Grass*. Bill, a conservative Ivy League professor, is drawn back to his small southern hometown to "not" aid his small-time pot-growing twin, Brady, in taking down a drug lord. Edward needed to look drastically different as he played both characters with the help of computer-generated effects. However, it was also imperative to him personally that he felt different so that he could construct speech patterns and mannerisms that would define each character. As is common in reality, someone's appearance illustrates character, and often, judgment is placed on that person's character before their true character emerges. Given the circumstances of the film, the conflicting characters of Bill and Brady, and the other characters they interact with, the drastic difference between the two brothers visually was important as assumptions about a character often led to deeper conflict and comedic situations that filled the theater with laughter.

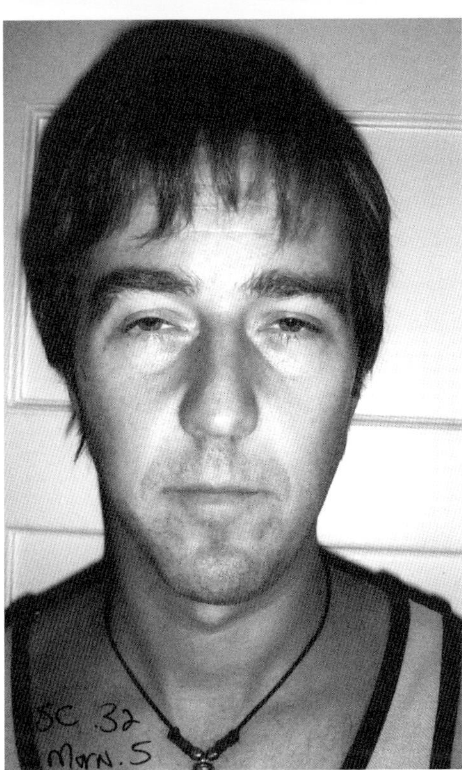

Edward Norton,
***Leaves of Grass*, 2009**

Brad Pitt, *Mr. & Mrs. Smith*, 2005

While the outer aspects of characters I have helped mold are essential, designing a hairstyle that extracts the character's inner conflict is the greatest challenge. They say great acting happens in the pause between words and sentences. At that moment, a viewer hangs in anticipation, and their eyes search the frame, analyzing the actor, the character, for anything that may reveal the thoughts processed in the lack of speech. Here, the character's look must reflect the unspoken emotional context. Natalie Portman displayed this so well in *Anywhere But Here*, with her consistent silence amid her mother's boisterous character, played by Susan Sarandon, and the inner conflict that often arises as she stews in the surroundings where she has been forced to exist. Her character is framed by an awkward wardrobe and hairstyles representing her mother's wishes rather than hers. Zooey Deschanel uses her amazing, big, blue eyes in varying degrees of shock and awe during *The Happening* as she tries to understand and avoid the menace of the unseen force overtaking the world. Unspoken sequences of sheer horror are framed with blunt bangs and long hair that falls close to her cheeks to accentuate the freneticism and horror her eyes beacon throughout the story. Tommy Lee Jones in *JFK* needed to hide his alter-ego of "Clay Shaw" for several reasons. He was a homosexual man at a time (the 1960s) when that was not considered acceptable by the elite society people of New Orleans. He was a respectable businessman who needed to be viewed as conservative and professional. Clay Shaw needed to be concealed behind the actual identity of the man, Clay Bertrand, so that he could conduct covert operations for the CIA and Cubans. Tommy Lee Jones adjusted the way he walked, carried himself, and his tone of speech in different scenes when he wished to accentuate character traits based on the persona with whom others were interacting in that situation. Watching Mr. Jones drift between the nuances of the character throughout that film was inspirational as he even incorporated the oppressive humidity of New Orleans we all had to endure that summer in 1990, something I could barely do with a fan in my hand and a cold towel around my neck.

I learned through interacting with all these actors and the metamorphosis we facilitated with wigs, mud, or hairpins that a person's appearance rarely defines that character. Character is developed by experience, interaction, and circumstance. I often recollect people who have come into my life and mentally reintroduce myself to that person to understand why they may have been the way they were or how they may have treated me, both positively and negatively. With these memories revisited, I often find that I am more accepting of the individual and our relationship; I am inclined to look at the positives from the negative instances, and I am more compassionate and accepting in the future. Audrey Hepburn once said, "Everything I learned, I learned from the movies." Even though I never attended college, if what Audrey claims is true, I should be awarded a bachelor's, master's, and doctorate for what I learned in Hollywood. I have used the knowledge I gained from studying characters to develop my own and helped others with their character development, sometimes without them needing to say a word.

REAL AND FICTIONAL CHARACTERS HAVE GUIDED ME TO BECOME THE PERSON I AM TODAY, MINUS THE VAMPIRE, THE SERIAL KILLER, AND THE ALIEN.

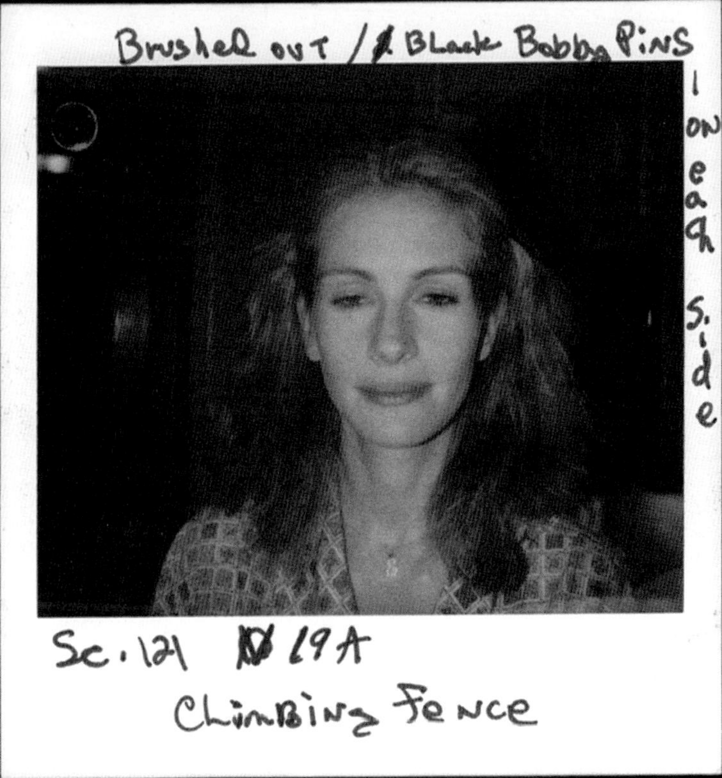
Brushed out / 1 Black Bobby Pins
1 on each side
Sc. 121 19A
Climbing Fence

06

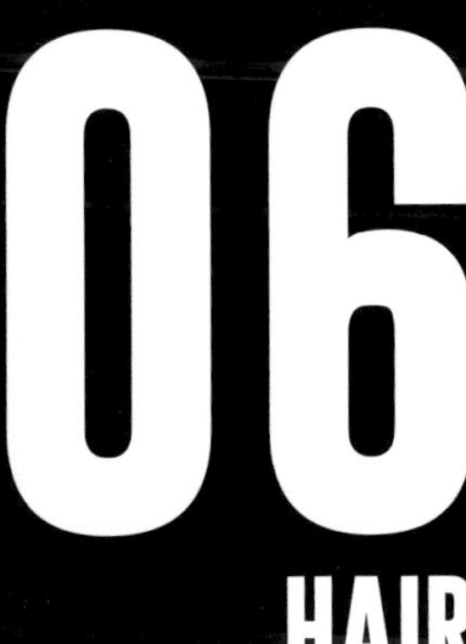

HAIR DRAMA

Years ago, I attended my son's wedding in Barcelona. Like so many other weddings performed that day around the world, the monumental day was marked with a photo slideshow on a big screen. The slideshow was a montage recollection of the lives the two individuals led apart for years, featuring photos from dating until they joined hands at the altar. Sports jerseys dated some photos, and others had eyeglasses that matched music trends on MTV, but what got all the laughs and brought all the smiles were the hairstyles that marked the milestones that led to that wonderful day.

Having a career that spans decades, I have not only seen nearly every hairstyle in history, but I have been responsible for portraying them on actors to convince audiences that the movie was filmed during prohibition in Chicago rather than last March in Milwaukee. There are even hairstyles that I have created that define non-fictional characters, and the hairstyles of Julia Roberts in *Erin Brockovich* are in an undefined category on their own. So, you would think that being an experienced hair stylist would make me sit up and take pride in the photos of my son in the montage shown that day. Instead, it had me cringing in my seat, covering my eyes at what next would be projected on screen to all the guests; questions of my talent echoed in their jeers as their jaws dropped frame after frame with each image of the wild hairstyles he had worn throughout the years.

My daughter was always the conservative one of my two children. She was ready to color and cut, perm, and straighten to fit in perfectly with a chorus line of drill team members or blend into every student body from grammar school throughout her years of attaining her master's degree. On the other hand, my son was always looking for the cutting edge of everything. Whether it was music, film, technology, or anything new and different, he had to reflect that in his clothes and, most of the time, his hair. And being the individual he is, when it came time to cut his hair, we had quarrels rivaling the Hatfields and McCoys. Instead of trimming the ends, which would take fifteen minutes, he would jump up from the chair and run to the mirror, yelling throughout the house that I was taking too much off with nearly every snip of the shears. At one point, I was so tired of the length he had grown his hair during his music business phase that I resorted to cutting off his ponytail in his sleep. I came to my senses and let him sleep, not because I was afraid of how he would feel about me but how he would think of himself. A few years in a hair salon was enough to teach me the importance of hair and how it defines a person's life.

When my husband, kids, and I moved to Indiana, I worked part-time at a salon in the L.S. Ayres Department Store. When they found out I had done hair for the movies, I quickly built my clientele of socialites and style seekers of all ages and hair types, despised by others who had worked in the salon for years. I quietly spent my days doing permanent waves, shampooing, setting frosted hair, and cutting in the latest fashions of the celebrities whose hair I had done. I crafted

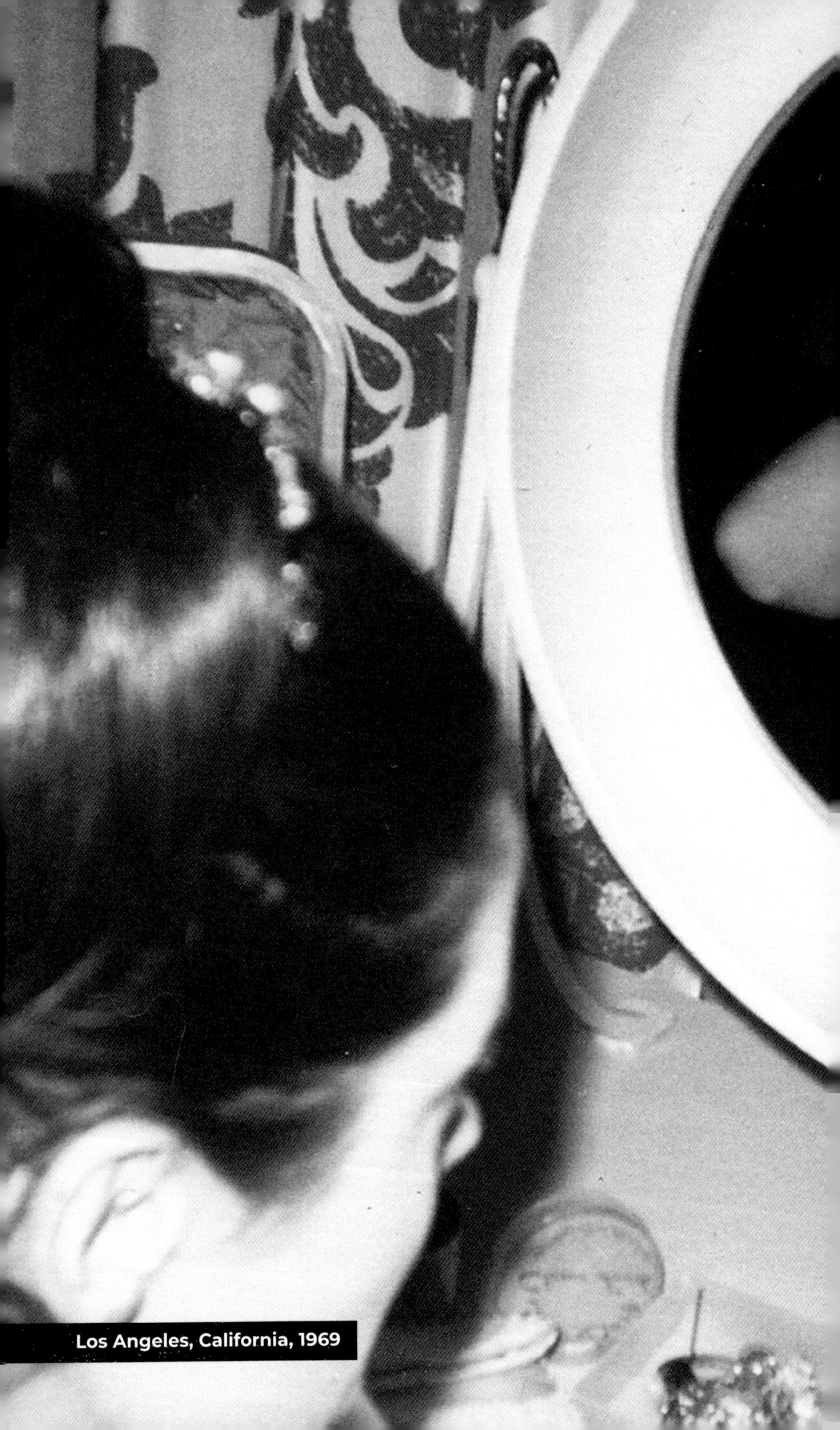

Los Angeles, California, 1969

coifs for brides-to-be and diamond anniversary dinners to be shared, proms, and parades that brought joy to the baton twirlers and people lining the streets of Memorial Circle. I also played rescue stylist for those needing to correct a mistake they had made themselves or trusted to the hands of a less-than-qualified stylist from another part of town. I developed an uncanny knack for taking a hair disaster from what was once a pumpkin of a cut and color into a brunette pixie envied at the country club. Standing behind a slouching teenager sobbing heavily hours before her winter formal because her perm rested in a clump on her shoulders, I watched her eyes dry, her shoulders pull back, and her smile beam as she exited the salon, slightly skipping, with blonde ringlets bouncing in the crisp December breeze.

I also learned to refine my skills as a hair therapist during those years at the salon. It's one thing to adjust to the manners and moods of an actor you have been working with for months. You note how they punch the keys more furiously when texting under stress, as Internet slang is misconstrued in a virtual conversation. When one actress becomes feistier at a particular time of the month, I look at my calendar, letting me know it's not about something I did but something that is generally out of her control. During filming, and especially with someone I have worked with on another production, I come to understand the subtle nuances of their natural character that lets me know when they need comforting work or when the situation will be lightened with a joke and when I should keep my mouth shut and just let them talk or scream or cry it out. A symbiosis develops between my actors and me, and we develop into a duet that can accomplish the scenes of a script and the screenplay of life in unison with just a few glances in the mirror during the early morning hours when we are alone.

Reading an actor and a friend that I am familiar with is one bag of tricks; discerning the mental makeup of a charity chairwoman who is thrust into mid-life psychosis when she sees herself disheveled in a salon mirror requires miracles on my part, reading deep between the lines on her scrunched forehead and the wrinkles in her writhing hands. It's akin to sizing up a boy who has just walked across a crowded party and asked you to dance. You have two seconds to listen to the confidence of his voice, or lack thereof, and to ascertain the amount of sweat in his palms as he daintily or definitively shakes your hand and decide whether you will make his night or smash his ego as you flip your bobbed hair and let your hips slide side to side as he watches you walk away. When a customer sits down in the chair, that first glance at them in the mirror lets you know if you are going to need to lightly dress the wound or prep them for surgery, as most people don't realize what they want, and if they do, it's many times for the wrong reason. My job is to read clients' minds, listen to their stories, and replicate some consistency in their mood all through the locks on their heads, whether thick with youth or straining with age.

A haircut or style is not about looking like Hilary Swank or Kristen Stewart. After all, a lot of the time, it's not even their real hair. Curling and blowing, spraying and teasing natural hair every day for months will compromise even the healthiest head of hair. We use hair lace wigs that cost thousands of dollars, extensions, and fake hair falls to create the masquerade of perfect hair and sometimes the illusion of not-so-perfect hair. A woman who enters any salon or tries out a new style should have her emotions and moments of her life mimicked through her hair. A hairstyle should complement your lifestyle and enhance your presence. I can tell when a woman is uncomfortable with her hair.

Julia Roberts, *Erin Brockovich*, 2000

Kurt Russell, *Captain Ron*, 1992

MOST BAD HAIRCUTS OR STYLES ARE NOT USUALLY BECAUSE OF THE STYLIST'S TALENT BUT RATHER THEIR LACK OF LISTENING AND FAILURE TO INTERPRET WHAT THE CLIENT IS FEELING OR THINKING.

She flings it back and forth, fidgeting with newly chopped bangs and stroking hair recently cut above the shoulders that now isn't there as she feels the void on the lapels of her jacket. But, when a woman has the right tresses, she passes a mirror, a moment of reflection of who she is in all her glory; when she walks into the room, party in full swing, she owns that room and the attention of everyone in it, especially her husband or boyfriend, communal rival, and the man in the corner looking for his path across the crowded room.

Standing behind many women, we stare at each other in the mirror, talking about everything from death to orgasms and all the other stuff life throws at us along the way, and I have always cherished that moment when I see a reflection begin to release the person it embodies, freeing them from life's tolls that have taken control. Emotions are emitted, and stress starts to fall away with each cluster of hair that is set free with my shears, inner beauty becoming outer realization in a smile, a little more laughter, and a confidence that swims deep in the eyes, catching a glance of one's true self, shining through from the soul. This moment happens with celebrities and "realities," as I call the greater population, and both are equally as rewarding, but none more so than when men do it.

I've run my fingers through the hair of more men than most women, including some of the most iconic men

Brad Pitt, *Mr. & Mrs. Smith*, 2005

Julia Roberts, *Confessions of a Dangerous Mind*, 2002

and heads of hair in movie history. I've defined them for generations for both sexes, introducing them to women I have never met and causing other men to mimic or mock them depending on the confidence of their masculinity. I find empowerment as a woman to know that I can use my hands to help men discover a strength or weakness in themselves that they had never identified just by cutting or combing their hair. A new hairstyle can make them look at their self-vision in a completely different light, especially when an actor creates a character that millions of people will know them as for eternity. After decades of doing my job, I am usually calm and collected, even when tousling Patrick Dempsey's dreamy hairdo. However, there have been a couple of occasions when I have feared doing anything to a man's hair, feeling that one wrong adjustment in length or switching the side of a hair part would be a series of events that would equate to stripping Samson of his strength, or in my case, the kingpin of machismo, Al Pacino, of his swagger.

While I enjoy watching many actors perform their craft and marvel at their ability to bring words to life as if they were born to play the role, I found myself in awe of every take as I watched Al Pacino in each film we worked on. The clap of an end-marker slate, slapping me into awareness that the camera had stopped rolling, was a regular occurrence in every film we worked on together. Having seen all his movies through the years, I figured his hair effortlessly followed him down the process of developing the look, voice, walk, and mannerisms of the characters he played. It wasn't until I was in his pre-production presence that I realized how meticulous and discerning he was when designing the hairstyle that would be the visual fiber of the character he would portray. Developing those looks for Al was always profound, as most of his characters are perceived, and our last film together would be a concluding statement to that intensity.

When we began preparing for his character in *Any Given Sunday*, I realized what he expected of himself, setting himself far above any other actor who had portrayed another football coach in some other sports movie.

Arriving at Oliver Stone's office that afternoon and having the relationship I have had for many years with that brilliant director, he knew how to get me ready for war, and I knew we were going into combat once again when he asked me in his gruff way, "Are you ready for this battle, Bonnie?"

I understood what Oliver meant the minute Al began speaking on the idea, and Oliver retorted with the opposite: the hair should be this way, and no, it should be this way, and then another idea that was opposite of the first, second, and third at the same time. I was in the middle, trying to decipher and mediate words and ideas between two creative minds that didn't see eye to eye. Al had aged, and his hair had begun to thin slightly, and here he was, trying to play a professional football coach in one of the most image-conscious cities in America: Miami. He wanted to be a hip, cool, strong, and somewhat sexy single man trying to fit in smoothly with the young players he was commanding rather than hanging out on the walls of the hall of fame with those who had reached their resting place. As we began to cut his hair, Al looked confused, bewildered by a part of his character that he couldn't figure out no matter what play he was running in his mind, hoping for an outcome that would counter anything that Oliver was throwing at him. We'd cut a little off the back, and Al would walk into the bathroom to look, coming back a little more convicted. Fumbling for a response, Oliver scrambled for a reason to contradict what had been handed to him visually. We'd take the sides in a little closer, and Al added a swagger to his walk, which was hipper and stoic. Oliver stopped pacing, surveying every inch of hair left on Al's head, the words not coming as fluently. So, when the top of Al's hair squared off, the character's metamorphosis was triumphant over the actor. Oliver slumped in his seat, arms folded in defeat, a single nod of the head in my direction that war had been won, and he had lost. Al straightened his suit jacket in the full-length mirror, turned to Oliver and me, held his hands out to his sides, and smiled that sly smirk, victorious.

The entire process of designing the look of Al's character would have been much easier if each of them had been saying precisely what they were thinking rather than talking in code as if they were calling offense and defense formations to throw the other off their plan.

I believe Oliver wanted to say, "Hey, Al, you're an older man, your hair isn't what it was, and let's chop it off and let you feel vulnerable like you are."

And knowing Al, he needed to demand, "Oliver, I am older, but you want me to feel as insecure as you do now that you don't have as much hair as you had when you were younger."

These hair metaphors represented everything the character sought: an unattainable life and career. The need to reestablish a sense of purpose in his life came from within rather than from the physical perception others had of him. When I watched that film, I didn't know the story's progression on the screen, but I saw the story and events unfolding that day in Oliver's office. The emotions unveil themselves and the transformation occurs when the character breaks down and realizes the facts about his age

Brad Pitt, *Mr. & Mrs. Smith*, 2005

and the playing field stacked against him. At that moment, the character that appears is a mold of the mannerisms and personality of the man himself, Al Pacino, and the reality of creating the character represented on screen.

These transformations occur in our real lives each day, and our responsibility to ourselves and those in our lives is to manage the incarnation of internal feelings with our external releases of annoyance and dissatisfaction in the form of crossed arms and winced eyes. Our instinct is to wear our emotions on our sleeves, camouflaged in between the patterns of dodging confrontation and not hurting feelings. We tap one foot when we are impatient instead of expressing our frustration directly. We roll our eyes when someone looks the other way because we are appalled by what they have said or done, rather than saying that we don't appreciate the course of action they chose. We have built our social communication structure on using emoticons and acronyms not only on cell phones but also in body positions and subtle gestures rather than speaking words and growing through communication, interaction, and honesty. Most of the arguments I have had with people over the years have been because of misinterpretations and failure to communicate appropriately. We tend to let our internal voices begin speaking over someone's words and comments, letting our thoughts and opinions form before we allow them to finish vocalizing their thoughts and feelings. As I have learned over the years, yet tend to forget from time to time, it's best to analyze what someone has said after they finish speaking rather than mid-sentence. This is essentially where life becomes a series of "good hair gone bad" moments.

Most bad haircuts or styles are not usually because of the stylist's talent but rather their lack of listening and failure to interpret what the client is feeling or thinking.

My dog, Wilma, in the trailer on the film *Little Man Tate*, 1991

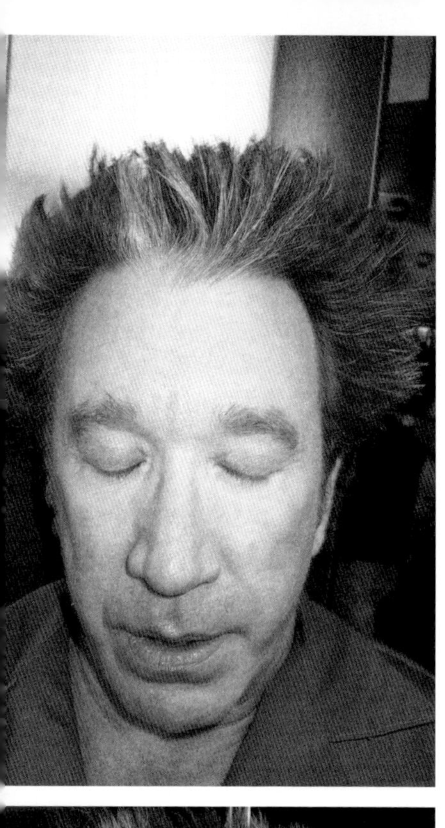

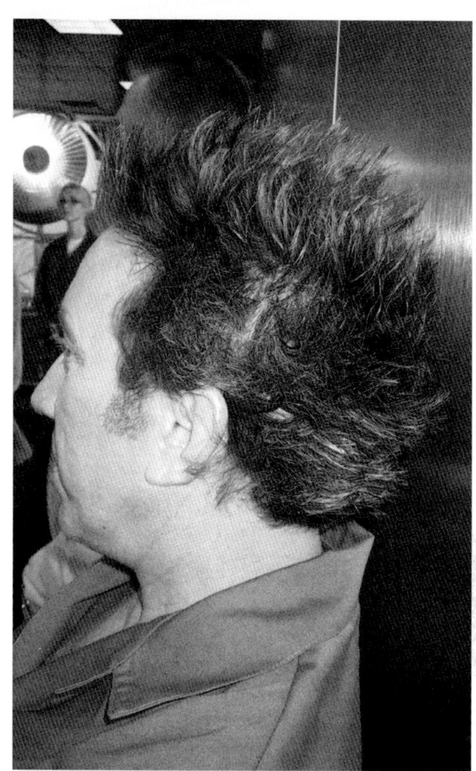

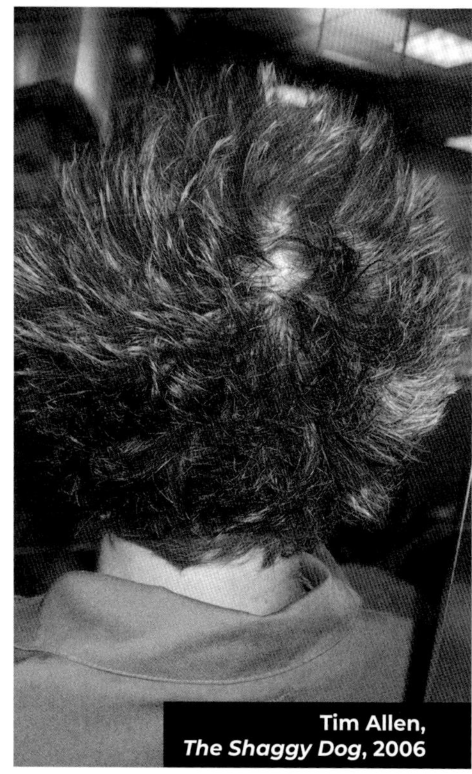

Tim Allen,
***The Shaggy Dog*, 2006**

Even though they speak the same language, the inflection in a person's voice who is troubled by a relationship or just lost their job is a different dialect than someone who just gave birth or won an award in their community. Translating monotone is the only successful way to turn bad hair moments into good. This pertains to someone sitting in my styling chair and every aspect of my life. When someone presents to me a problem, a concern, or a venting of a sort, I listen to their words, not their voice. People may change the tone or accentuate a conversation with hand gestures to make an even bigger point of something trivial, but their words will always tell me exactly what I need to know, how to react, and what words I should choose in response. Bad haircuts, colors, or styles usually result not from a lack of talent or uncertainty in choice but rather from a misread need and miscommunication of want. Success comes from taking those moments of miscommunication and treating the solution with patience, understanding, humility, and harmony. There is a give and take from both sides and a common ground that must be met to achieve a common goal. Radical, immediate adjustments never last and almost always cause more significant problems. If someone comes to me with a bad perm, the answer is not to straighten the hair because the result will look like a cat that got its tail stuck in an electrical socket, and there is a good chance the hair will split and break off, resembling a chia pet that met a weed whacker. I listen to the story of why they have this situation on top of their head, what words were exchanged with the previous stylist, and what their intentions are for stepping into a salon in the first place, maybe a first date or a slice of spice to a marriage that has moved way beyond the honeymoon phase. I let them speak their words, then gently help them realize what they meant and begin to work. I relax the curl, add layers underneath, and use a large curling iron to add wave. The final result is satisfaction on both our faces and a relationship that usually lasts through the next issue in life or a beauty need that arises.

However, not every bad hair day has a good one in response, and when those days come, my main focus is to make it until tomorrow or the next day, but never let the situation continue without taking action. This doesn't necessarily mean solving the entire problem, but at least making the best of a situation until you can change what is wrong at the root of the problem. This has happened in my family with quarrels I know are best to mask with a smile rather than discuss the entire issue between cutting the turkey and putting the whipped cream on the pumpkin pie at Thanksgiving. The problem with a sibling is something that wouldn't change overnight, and it was better to comfort them and suffice their needs for the sake of everyone else and then deal with them after the holidays when there was more time to focus on the core of their issue. This made the best of a situation that happened in a few films where I was brought in to fix a problem with a character's hair that didn't look just right to the director, especially the producers, and, more importantly, the actors themselves. Most recently, this occurred on one of the biggest franchises in modern movie history.

A month into filming *The Twilight Saga: Eclipse*, I was called in to figure out how to make Kristen Stewart's wig appear more natural and comfortable for her. She had finished filming *The Runaways*, in which she had extremely short punk rocker hair, and as Bella Swan, she needed long, flowing locks of wavy hair to match the character from the previous films. It wasn't necessarily the construction of the wig or the talent of the previous hair stylist, and Kristen can bear nearly any amount of discomfort for the sake of the film, but rather, it was a culmination of situations and

Julia Roberts, *Ocean's Eleven*, 2001

problems that led to the hand I had been dealt with this dilemma. Rather than reshooting scenes and scrapping the entire wig, I made adjustments and shot from various angles to make it look as good as possible. When it came time for *The Twilight Saga: Breaking Dawn*, we reassessed the situation, readjusted the techniques, and the hair looked fantastic. Kristen was comfortable with the hair's look and feel, and so were the producers, director, and everyone else with an opinion. The lesson we all learned was to make the best of a situation without sacrificing professionalism and then choose the appropriate moment when we can make everything better. This was made possible with patience, understanding, communication, and all parties willing to compromise. These are all the requirements for turning bad hair into good and, in turn, enabling life to turn from worse to better in due time.

As always, in all my trailers on movie sets, there comes a time to clear everything out, pack it up, and ship it somewhere else. Before I leave, one of the last things I do is take down the pictures I posted on the mirrors. Those photos cover several years and a variety of hairstyles of family and friends. Before leaving set in London in the fall of 2011, I removed several pictures of my son and laughed at how I chose photos where his hair was a style I approved.

It wasn't until someone who knew him saw the images in a stack that they said, "These don't look like your son at all."

After all, they knew him with hair past his shoulders when he was in the music business or spiked blonde hair when he was a fashion photographer. I realized at that moment that the images I posted were my vision of my son or, rather, glimpses of his life that satisfied my thoughts about how he should look. The photos didn't show my son as anyone else knew him, especially not as he knew himself. I realized that what we want to see is usually on the surface, like a haircut, clothes, or lipstick shade. However, what we need to see is below the surface, and when we discover that about a person, the relationship forms, solidifies, and endures. Those are the relationships we all strive for, and I only need to play a DVD of one of the films I have worked on to be reminded of the pride I have inside for forming many great relationships in my lifetime. As life has grown longer, I have slowly become more accepting of what I think of my son's hair, and it is mostly all good, but that still doesn't mean I can't tell him what I want.

AFTER ALL, I AM HIS MOTHER AND A HAIRSTYLIST, AND HE CAN'T WIN ANY ARGUMENT WITH THAT COMBINATION.

07 WHEN TO WALK OUT THE DOOR

THERE ARE ESSENTIALLY TWO TYPES OF CELEBRITIES: PROFESSIONALS AND AMATEURS.

STAGE DOOR

By now, you are probably wondering if I have anything bad to say about anyone I have worked with in Hollywood. Sure, there are petty things that colleagues or celebrities do that rile my skin and even sometimes put me on the verge of madness. But all in all, I have been very fortunate to work with a cast of characters in my life on and off the set who are so down to earth that if they weren't seen on TV and in magazines carrying Oscars and had their faces shown on billboards all over the world, you would never be able to pick them out of a lineup. I am also the type of person who avoids conflict, as I look at the importance of speaking my mind before opening my mouth and deciding whether it's worth all the problems that a few phrases could cause for a false sense of empowerment of getting the last word in. When someone goes off blaming me or someone else for anything that makes them feel better or covers up the problems that are rooted in their mental needs, I remember what a friend of mine once said, "If someone is pointing a finger at you, there are four more pointing right back at them."

There are essentially two types of celebrities: professionals and amateurs. I have tended to work with the former and, at all costs, avoided the latter both in productions and in social circles. To clarify, an amateur isn't necessarily someone who just started in the business. I've seen a couple of amateurs who have Oscars, and there is nothing more poisonous for the well-being of an entire production than an amateur in front of the camera. An amateur may be a great actor, but they are so concerned with industry status and personal perception by others that they cast aside any chance at nurturing relationships personally and professionally on and off the set. During the midst of production, many relationships need a lot of care for everyone to work together and produce a great film. These amateurs bring a sense of entitlement with them each day on set, and they put themselves above everyone else, thinking that they are better than anyone else at everything else. An amateur is usually clueless about what they are doing to an entire production unless the production lets them know straightforwardly, leaving little to interpretation.

I have seen this direct approach to terminating the amateur behavior of an actor in the most creative and shocking method I could ever imagine. It was working on the first Robocop film. Everything about the production was new and fascinating, filled with technology that I did not understand, and neither did many others on the crew, including the actors, from time to time. It was the first set I worked on with blue screens, and I was trying to imagine how a single color could be linked to a computer in post-production to produce the futuristic backgrounds of the world that the director, Paul Verhoeven, had visualized with his crew. It was something my imagination couldn't wrap around. While Peter Weller, the actor playing the character of *Robocop*, had to endure long, action-packed days in a heavy plastic and metal suit dodging gun blanks and squibs exploding on him as if the suit was deflecting incoming bullets in the suffocating heat of Dallas and Pittsburgh, he

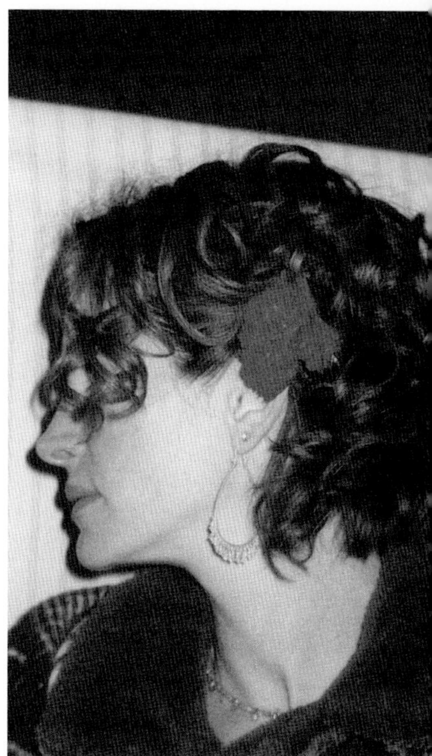

Julia Roberts,
The Mexican, 2001

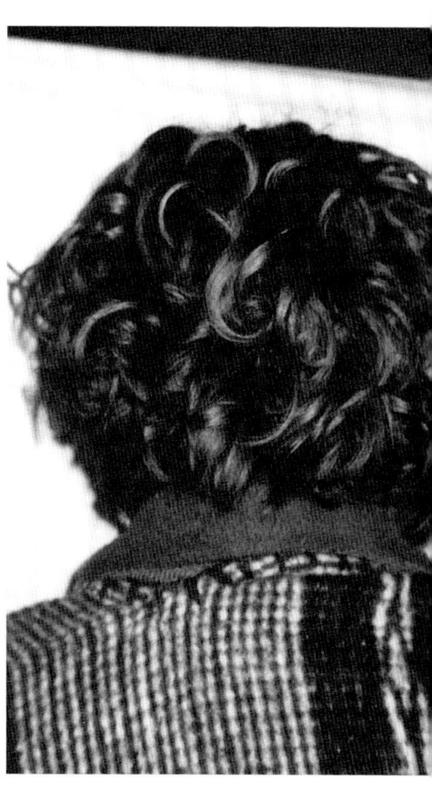

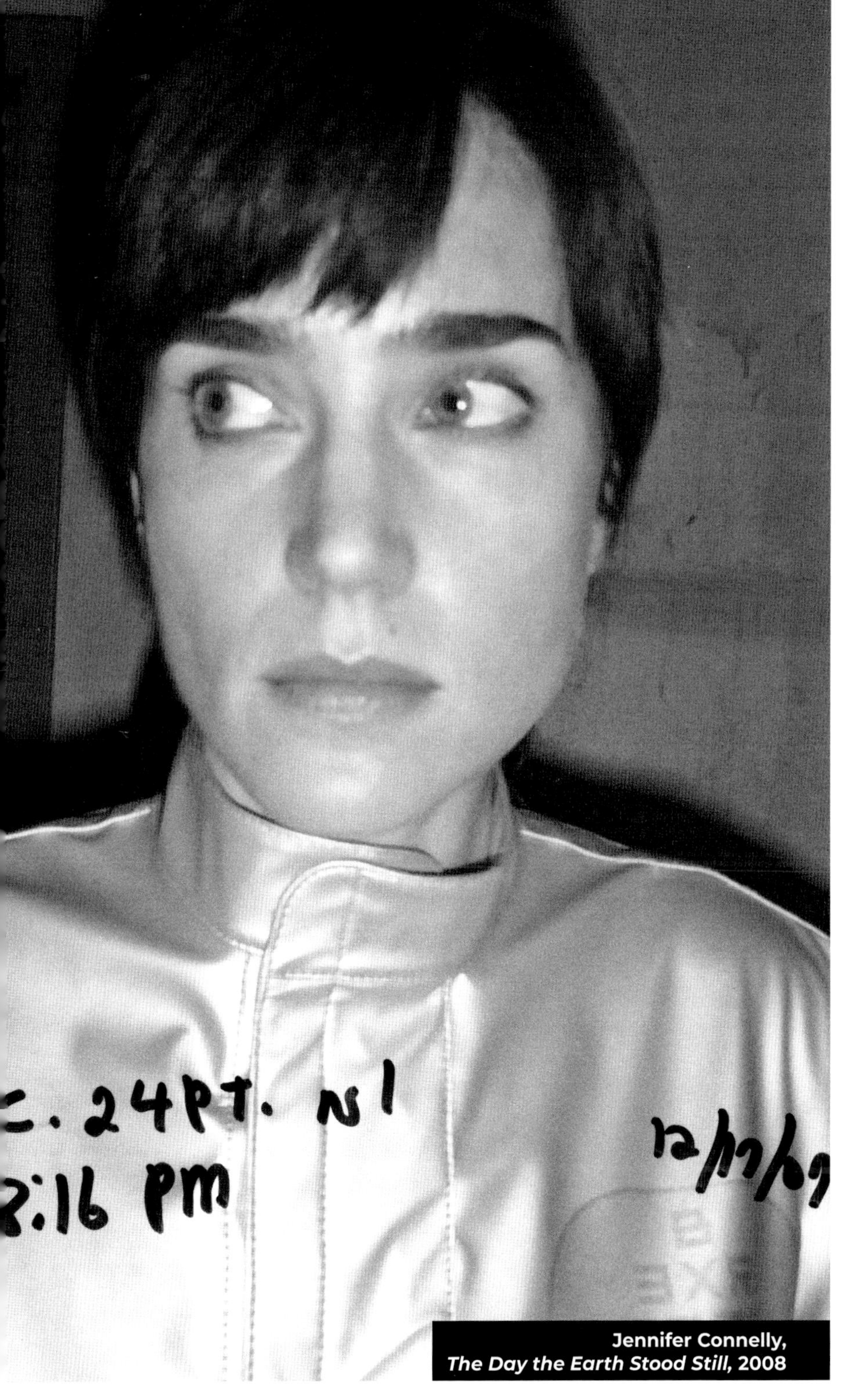

Jennifer Connelly,
***The Day the Earth Stood Still*, 2008**

had come across to much of the crew as a prima donna. I am sure he was exhausted from the long days and the physical toll that the suit and the action scenes took on his body and mind. He was always cordial to me, but word was circling the set that his comments and attitude were more than anyone working the same hours or more as Peter had to endure. According to nearly everyone on the crew sheet, Peter was an amateur and needed a wake-up call before the whole production cried mutiny. Near the end of shooting in an abandoned steel factory outside of Pittsburgh, the special effects team assembled the entire crew near a large pool of water with a metal and rock island in the center where they had placed something personal of Peter's. When he arrived at the gathering, everyone pointed out his director's chair, which was sitting alone with his name on it. Then, the director's chair exploded. It was not a tiny explosion but an action movie detonation that sent Peter's chair high into the air, crashing back to earth in a cauldron of smoke and flames. As the crew began to cheer and clap, Peter stood dumbfounded for only a moment. The message began to take solid form in his mind, and his recollection of the weeks passed immediately brought his attitude into check. I remember him nodding his head with acknowledgment and tiptoeing to his trailer to slip out of the Robocop suit. When he returned to work the next day, he was full of compliments for the crew and smiles for those who had helped him become one of cinema's most memorable action figures. Peter Weller had always been a great actor, but after that incident, he realized what an amateur was and became a professional in my eyes.

Then there is the type of celebrity I have been fortunate to work with most of my career: the professional. These actors get the job done no matter what it takes, their relationship status that day, or how much discomfort they may have from a common cold or an injury sustained. They suppress their fears and hold back their personal perils because they know they can adapt all those experiences and emotions into constantly evolving layers of complexity. The character they play needs to make us believe they can conquer monsters, defeat the odds, and even endure an evil witch's curse. I have often been amazed at what an actor goes through to complete the character and fulfill the requirements of a scene, but when that actor is a five-foot-four, twenty-one-year-old girl, I am even more amazed. While

---

WITHOUT SELFISHNESS, WE LISTEN A LITTLE LONGER, CARE MORE INTENSELY, AND OPEN OUR MINDS TO BIGGER PROSPECTS AND OPPORTUNITIES.

---

filming *Snow White and the Huntsman*, Kristen Stewart showed me the strength and professionalism she exudes beyond her age, more so than any other woman beyond her years or physically superior man I have ever seen.

While playing Snow White, Kristen had a couple of instances of just sheer bad luck, leaving her going to the emergency room twice for her tiny wrist that had its tendons pulled and strained during battle scenes on horseback and fleeing angry soldiers down a slippery Welsh hillside. She wore a brace on her forearm for several weeks, finally casting it aside because it interfered with her performance, and her pain was not as important as the film's final result. Through the chill and rain, Kristen kept nodding yes as her body shivered in the London fog. If there was another take, then so be it. When she was coughing considerably from a cold that had consumed most of the crew, she climbed up a set of stairs, rushed out of a cave on a cliff, and jumped

Jennifer Aniston, *Office Space*, 1999

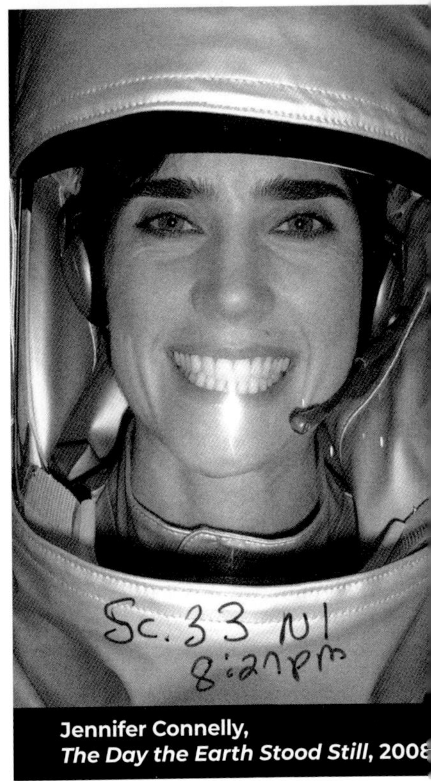

Jennifer Connelly,
***The Day the Earth Stood Still*, 2008**

fifteen feet into a tank of freezing water, not once, but every time the director asked to her swim in that chilly pool. From the first time we worked on *The Twilight Saga: Eclipse* to this very day, I am amazed at how she doesn't need awards or the praise of peers to know, personally, that she is a professional.

Kristen Stewart was not the only one on that set with an injury. I was seventy-one years old, and as much as I tried to protect what was left of my body, the pieces were starting to wear and wither a little bit more with every production. After filming *The Twilight Saga: Breaking Dawn 1 and 2* over six consecutive months, my shoulder began progressively hurting more and more. I tried homeopathic remedies and massage therapy before I would finally succumb to scans and x-rays that would reveal I had a list of injuries that included tears and bone fragments floating through my tissues. Knowing that I had to attend both of my children's weddings and immediately begin production in London, I thought I would be as professional as possible and get through the production no matter the pain. With the assistance of a great hair department and Kristen's understanding and patience, I fought each day to hide my pain until I could get home and crawl into bed. Week after week, the pain got worse and worse, but I continued to work, putting everyone and everything in front of the discomfort I felt from the first scene to the last. A few times, as the temperature dropped while filming nights, I thought about leaving the show, but I knew that it would only let everyone else down, and that's not what being a professional is about, so I continued through to the end. I know there is a time to walk out the door, and my body each morning said it wasn't that time. I had only left a production twice. Once, when my husband became ill a short time before he passed away, not knowing at the time the outcome of his health, I was devastated to leave my actors behind in the production. The second time was the only time I left a film because of the antics and attitude of an actor, and little did I know that one of the most revered female legends in Hollywood would turn out to be the one that made me realize the importance of knowing when to walk out the door.

Like any healthy relationship, my husband and I fought for many reasons. Money, the kids, our schedules, with whose family to spend the holidays—you name it, we fought about it. What I learned from all those years and countless fights was when to walk out the door, take a drive, sit in the park, anything to diffuse how I felt, let him do the same, and then return much more rationally than either of us had started out and escalated to in our quarrel. I knew when words were being used to be hurtful, and rather than both of us saying anything we would regret, the best step was to back out of the room and let the dust settle. I applied what I learned at home to my life, especially my career. I knew when somebody wasn't in a good mood on a set to put my chair in a secluded corner to remove me from the tension. When somebody told me how to do my job, I stood my ground to the point that their argument was irrational. I walked out of the room, let them realize or clarify their position, and then came back and collaborated until we both were satisfied. That method of slipping away until I could return with strength and resolve worked for three decades in the film business until I got called with what I thought was a dream job, but that turned into a nightmare of one week when I learned more about something I had never realized was so important in life. There is a time when you need to walk out the door and never turn back.

When I was called to work with Academy Award winner Faye Dunaway, in my excitement, I forgot what they were calling the two-hour *Columbo* TV movie. After my experience and all these years later, I still cannot bear to utter that film's title. Having admired her work on *Mommy Dearest* and almost everything else she had done, I was thrilled to be given the opportunity to work with some of her professionalism, or so I thought. When you have been in the industry long enough, you hear stories of other productions and people involved that let you know what to expect from someone who might be difficult to work with. The stories I had heard of Faye could never have prepared me for what I was about to go through and the lesson I ultimately learned.

I was summoned to Ms. Dunaway's house a few days before shooting. I imagined a lavish estate perched on the hillside overlooking the whole of Hollywood. Walking into the house, I realized I was walking into the drama queen's castle, and with her dismissive hello, I was introduced to the truth behind all the tales I had heard. I followed her into her dressing room, carrying my equipment: a hair dryer, multiple-size curling irons, assorted brushes and combs, and a small beauty supply store of products for every hair type. Laid out on the table in rigid and particular order were nearly the exact tools I had brought, and I began to settle that I was on the same page as Faye. The problem was that her page was white, and mine was black, which was the first but not the last moment we didn't see eye to eye. She explained why she used each item and in what specific manner it was to be used, telling me the same instructions over and over as if explaining the rules of kindergarten to a child. When I would acknowledge an understanding of what I already knew, Faye took that as I wasn't listening,

Brad Pitt and Julia Roberts, *The Mexican*, 2001

interrupting her lesson, and she began her explanation over again. As she carefully replaced each brush and comb, product and utility to its position on the table, slightly adjusting the item until it was perfectly spaced from the others, she would pause in uncomfortable silence, smiling blankly at me, trying to read if I had fallen under her spell, subservient to her every request and need.

Over the first week of filming, Faye Dunaway continued her lessons every morning. She continued throughout the day, a parochial schedule of classes in hairstyling, a craft in which I had amassed more than forty filmmaking credits at that time and of which I believed I had a firm understanding. She would push and pull her hair, causing me to push and pull it in another direction until she got frustrated, and we nearly started from scratch. We spent hours and hours in the trailer trying to perfect the imperfect because, in her eyes, I would never be good enough for her, which was set in her mind many times before, as colleagues had warned me. Still, I just had to go through it myself to believe that she could really make me feel like I couldn't live up to her expectations. On the first Friday of filming, I did something I had never done in my career before or after that date. I packed all my equipment, loaded my car, notified the production manager, and quit. My husband helped me carry my cases up to our apartment and held me close as I cried a long while, comforting me in my decision with the simple words, "No job is worth losing yourself over."

The next day, the doorbell rang, and standing there was a delivery boy hidden by the most massive display of floral arrangements I had ever seen. I invited him in, steadying his struggle up the stairs, where he placed the vase with a thud on the dining room table. Given the value of the flowers and the film's budget, I knew they were sent by the only one on that crew who could afford this many lilies and white roses.

The note card read in a flamboyant script of cursive ink, "Please accept my apology, Faye."

While I appreciated the gesture, the sting had already poisoned any idea I had of trying to make amends when she called later that evening. I had one of the most respected motion picture hair stylists over for dinner that night, and as we discussed the past week's events, the phone rang.

Before I could answer, the voice on the other end of the line softly spoke, "Hello, it's Faye."

Having been the second youngest in my family, a wife for thirty years, and a mother of two, I know when an apology is sincere and when someone is apologizing to justify their actions to themself. This was the latter, and I expected a much more believable performance from an Academy Award winner. I listened through her entire monologue and told her I appreciated her words and gift, but I had a dinner guest. When I mentioned my guest's name, whom Faye knew very well, she abruptly changed her tone.

She blurted the final line of her soliloquy, "Well, I know what the conversation at that table is going to be about." She terminated the phone call, and the din of the dial tone reinforced my resolve regarding my decision the day before.

The lesson I learned is a cautious one, and I have never used it again in the film business, only in my personal life. I have always been the last to throw in the towel in every aspect of relationships, but I know when to walk out the door. Whether it is tough love for one of my children who

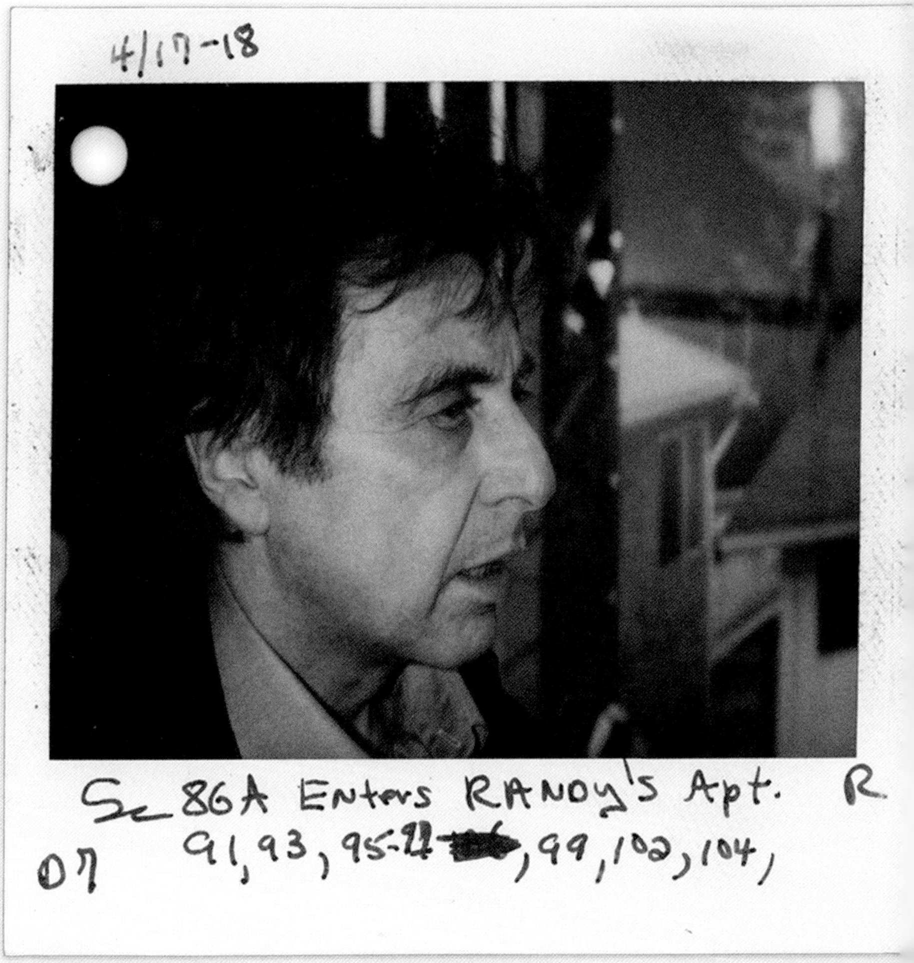

4/17-18

Sc 86A Enters RANDY'S Apt. R

D7 91, 93, 95-97, 99, 102, 104,

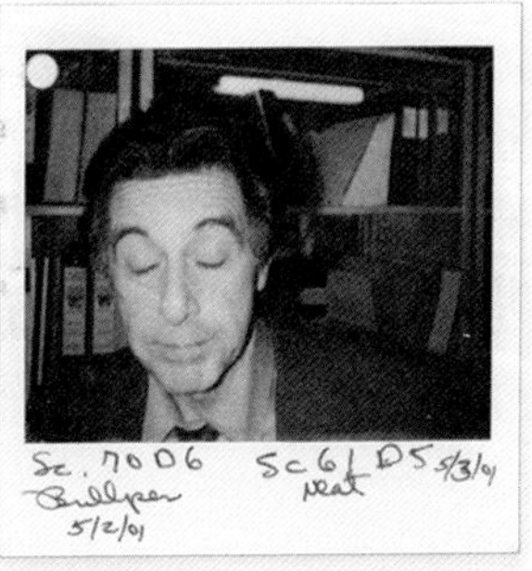

Al Pacino, *Insomnia*, 2002

needs to learn life's lessons on their own or a sibling who feels that their feelings are the only one that matters, I know that the more I try to convince them otherwise, my absence, even briefly, is the only way they will be able to realize their foils. That's not to say I am always right, as I am rarely, but when someone disregards your opinion for the sake of argument, demeans your ability, or is hurtful toward you for their own self-gratification, that is the time to walk out the door. In most cases, that doesn't mean forever, but just long enough for you to realize that either you are misguided in your ways or to understand that the other person needs something emotionally, physically, or mentally that you can't provide.

Years later, I look back on all the arguments I have seen happen on set; some were solved with an explosion, others had an exit stage left, but all had a common theme. They all began and ballooned because someone was being selfish. In my opinion, selfishness is one of the biggest flaws of human beings. Without selfishness, we listen a little longer, care more intensely, and open our minds to bigger prospects and opportunities. I have seen what happens when selfishness destroys the essence of creativity. When it is absent from production, the movie magic flourishes into a beautiful experience both on set and on the screen. I relish those films where selfishness is put on hold, and we, as artists, can give all our talent to a common cause. Most of the films I have worked on have been unselfish experiments in artistry and innovation, and they are lessons and memories in my life that I translate each day into a mental mantra that keeps me from walking out the door.

It's hard to believe that in all the years of working in the film business, which can be as catty as a sorority house during rush, I don't have more stories to tell about celebrities and crews, for the simple reason that I wouldn't want to face them if they found out what I had said. Little did I know I would have to face the one and only person I had said something negative about years ago. I was beginning another film and looking at the cast and crew call sheet when her name caught my eyes in shock and horror. In bold type near the middle of the page, Faye Dunaway's name stared back at me, ready to reenact her revenge. I spent the first few days finding hiding places all over that set, planning my entrances and exits like an escape from Alcatraz. I felt my hiding routine was down to perfection when I was alone in the trailer one day, and the door swung open. There she stood, oblivious to who I was, only searching for her hairstylist, whom she needed to teach a lesson again. As I crouched in my chair, letting my hair fall in my face, I prayed she wouldn't catch my reflection in the mirror. I mumbled that I had no idea where her prey had gone. I thought I had cloaked myself well enough as she turned and began to exit. As I peeked to see if she had left, and our eyes met, her pirouette back toward me indicated that I might have been found out. She studied me quizzically, knowing without knowing if we had met before as she politely asked me. When I responded that we had worked briefly on a film before, the memories flooded back and flushed the rose from her cheeks. Her blank face was only punctuated by the v-line wrinkles that unhappily formed between her brows. Without a word, she turned again on her heels and left. I laughed heartily to myself when the door slammed closed, knowing the lessons from years before had come full circle.

I GUESS FAYE HAD ALSO LEARNED WHEN TO WALK OUT THE DOOR.

Sc 122 D20 Pool/ Frog
123 ↓ water sample / Hinkley Well
124 " " " "
125 " " " "

08

Brad Pitt and Julia Roberts, *The Mexican*, 2001

It was the winter of 1956 when I first fell in love with someone I never had a chance with at all. He was a few years older, but I saw him often while riding the bus; a discarded newspaper displayed his latest achievement in full color, which, at that time, was reserved for only the greatest of honors. Probably due to the depth of my crush, it seemed he was everywhere I turned. He was the topic of conversation among my friends in the malt shop and between classes, and I was jealous when I saw another girl twirling her bubble gum adoringly when she spoke his name. I learned very little during the spring of '57 because entire classes were occupied by me doodling our first names joined in holy matrimony, every combination of our last names written with and without my maiden name hyphenated. No matter how sweaty I was, he was always at my locker when I returned from P.E. When I fell asleep at night, he was there to watch me close my eyes and drift into a dreamy slumber. We had picnics near the creek and took long walks through the park, holding hands and fawning into each other's eyes. The problem was that he lived two thousand miles away in a city I would not live in for another two decades. As much as he was in every moment of my existence for a few years, Paul Newman lived only in magazines, pictures, posters, and movies. I was left alone to

(Left Page to Right Page):
Michael Douglas, *Traffic*, 2000;
Peter Falk, *Tune in Tomorrow*, 1990

BECAUSE OF MY FATHER, I LEARNED EARLY ON THAT WOMEN'S VIEWS ABOUT MEN MUST BE REALISTIC IN ORDER TO KEEP SANE.

---

fantasize about when we would meet and get married, like every other schoolgirl in America.

As young girls, we have expectations of men that are absolute fantasies that, for me, started to dwindle into stark reality at too young an age. While I went to the theater every Saturday that I could afford to ogle and gawk at my idea of the perfect man, when I returned home, I was brought to my senses as my father came into view. He would be sitting in the front yard, smoking his cigar, not a word out of his mouth as he let me pass by, exhaling heavily, the weight of the world more unbearable with the birth of each child. My father was a loving man in his own way, but not in the way that a girl nearing her teens envisions a man being to anyone, including his children. And while my father passed away 37 years ago, he continually influenced my expectations of men. I quickly evolved into a young woman who viewed men as manipulators, my father being more Boris Karloff than Bing Crosby. But those stars that made me swoon, a reverie of a need that was eluding my childhood, also made me realize that it didn't hurt to dream but was impossible to expect. Because of my father, I learned early on that women's views about men must be realistic in order to keep sane.

I began dating as a teenage woman, looking for physical characteristics in men opposite my father, hoping the visual would mask my misconceptions of men. I dated every type of guy, whether short and stout or tall and slim, anything different from my father, at least enough for a first date. What I slowly came to realize was that my father wasn't the only one to blame. My mother had a hand in my perception of men, as every time my father would begin one of his rants, my mother would cringe and sweep the entire incident under the rug the next day. Back then, women didn't speak up, which was our house's cardinal sin of subservience. Her intentions to avoid conflict lasted nearly her entire life until she died at ninety-nine years old. Her request for our silence as children under challenging matters of our lives kept a traumatizing event in my youth a personal secret for most of my life.

I wouldn't say I dated a lot, but I caught the eyes of a few more than they saw mine. One thing led to another, and I began dating a politician's son in Illinois. He was from a wealthy family, handsome and groomed for politics, from how he dressed, how he walked, and especially how he talked. Every syllable was a slippery stretch of the truth. But I was enchanted with everything he had and said, and though I never deserved what he did to me, I could have been wiser to the snake that seduced me into his car that night. Writhing across the pleather seats, grasping for a door handle just out of reach, the convertible sealed tight enough to muffle my screams as his hands thwarted my every attempt to resist. Slipping into shock, the pain slightly stifled as it was coursing through my body, the car rocking back and forth silently, faintly illuminated by a streetlamp on a suburban street amidst cookie-cutter houses and tall oak trees.

The following day, I woke up and began doing what my mother had taught me so well. I systematically started to make excuses for myself, blaming my gullible innocence; I pulled out my mental broom and proceeded to sweep the entire incident under the rug, knowing that if I broke my silence, the first person who wouldn't believe me would be my mother. Decades later, during lunch one day, I put down my fork, and the words began to slide out of my mouth. I explained what had happened and how I had kept it inside, as far away from her as possible, because that was what I was taught.

Suddenly, she stopped me in mid-sentence with a quick exclamation, "I don't want to hear about this," and then went right back to shoveling her Chinese chicken salad into her mouth to stop her words from escaping. Her mother had long ago taught her, and her mother's mother, that men were put on this earth for a woman's protection and convenience and that women had a societal responsibility to serve men. We finished lunch in silence. Afterward, she lay down for a nap, and I stroked her silver hair, knowing there was no way she could change her views or comfort me. I, on the other hand, hadn't learned anything. Unfortunately, I was reminded to keep my mouth shut and push it all further into my silence, my resolve being that I would pass a very different lesson down to my daughter. I am proud to say that, as a mother, my daughter doesn't have a proverbial broom or rug in sight.

Today, things are no different than they were back in the '40s and '50s. The media purveys an ideal about male and female relationships that is less tangible than the paper on which it is printed. The Internet is filled with blogs and posts discussing empowerment and how men should treat women. These discussions are unrealistic and unlikely to survive beyond the first date. The fashion magazines demand that we be placed on a pedestal and put our men on leashes as if they were dogs, but this is only valid when we treat them as such. All the while, we listen to

Charlie Sheen and D.B. Sweeney, *Eight Men Out*, 1998

these relationship fables and baseless wisdom, wandering through the majority of our lives not looking at what we want from a man: someone with whom we can share our life side by side, needing to be needed and wanting to be comforted, while recognizing that we are fundamentally contradicting and respecting each other for and despite such disparities. I've seen these themes in movies over time, and I have worked on many through the years that reflect the times and the expectations of relationships between men and women in real life, told from a perspective that fills seats with the promise of laughing at ourselves and sometimes inciting us to change the way we perceive each other. It wasn't until after I had worked on many movies that I finally realized how my actual life influenced the characters' lives that I created for the films I worked on. The real-life story of a movie called *Eight Men Out* would awaken me to this truth by causing me to face in a frightening way what had been lingering in my mind in memories of my youth and realities of my present that would affect my future in the years to come, both personally and professionally.

Eight Men Out is the factual account of the 1919 Chicago "Black Sox" baseball team accused of conspiring to fix the World Series. The film was shot in a minor league stadium around Indianapolis in the late 1980s. When I sat down to design the look of the film, I went through old family albums, looking at photos of relatives and my parents in their youth. As I sat there thumbing through countless pictures of days gone by, I continued past the period of the film and looked at my family evolve through the decades, the dresses I remembered, and the hairstyles that defined the eras in which we grew up. After we began to film, I felt uneasy in the recollection of looking through all those family albums, lingering in my mind that something was not right with the look of the film. Something bothered me in a way I couldn't place a finger on until I remembered the root of the annoyance. Whether it was the period and all the actors in period haircuts with their banded straw hats and snappy double-breasted suits or when I was filming *Eight Men Out*, my father's ghost seemed to be in each screaming voice and every angered face. Staring into the stands of Triple-A ballpark in Indianapolis, the hundreds of extras dressed in wardrobe and shouting back at the field in unison, a chorale group of voices funneled into the sound I heard come out of my father's mouth when he drank a little too much and let us all know who ruled his house. Unbeknownst to me consciously, I had designed an entire look for every male character to look like my father, from the early ages of the ball players to the elderly newspaper writers. I was haunted for the entire filming, and it was mostly my fault. Even though the actors were warm and cordial every day we worked together, Charlie Sheen and

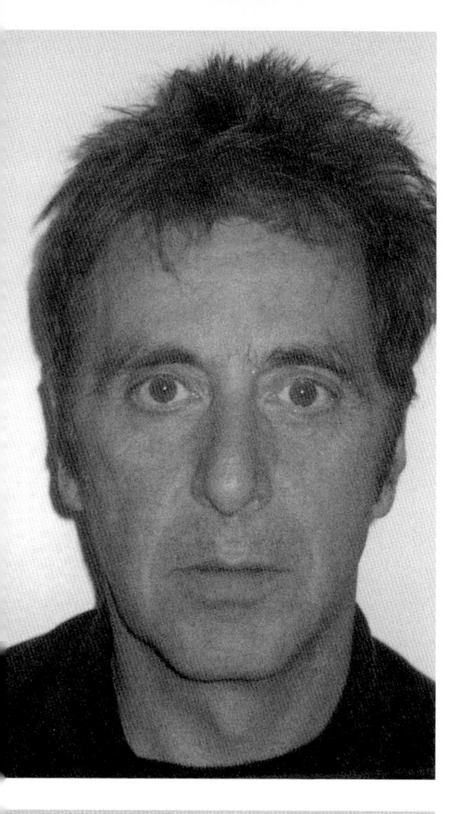

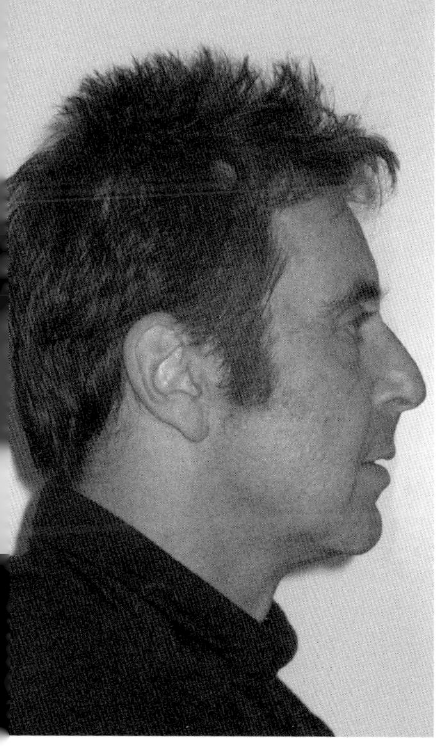

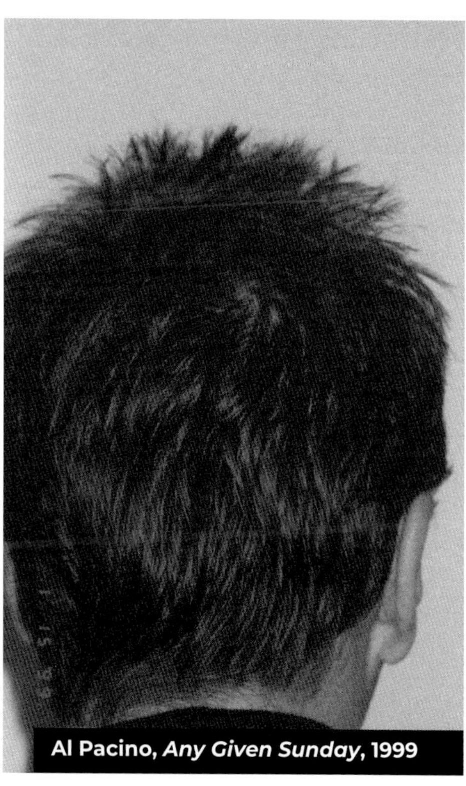

Al Pacino, *Any Given Sunday*, 1999

John Cusack were my father at twenty-five, John Sales was my father at forty-five, and Michael Lerner was my father at sixty. Although their voices and faces differed, I couldn't help but recognize little nuances in their performance that brought me back to moments in my life that I did not care to relive.

Unlike many of the films that I have watched time and time again with friends and family, proud of the work and appreciative of the praise, *Eight Men Out* is one of the few I change the channel on any time it reruns on television. I look back and determine what caused me to recreate my father in an entire cast. Maybe it was because I missed him, as he had passed away only a couple of years previously. Although the emotional bruises of growing up under his roof mainly had healed as I had dealt with a new definition of family men in my husband and son, I recollect now that possibly I wanted to be confronted with the fears and disillusions my father had created in me that I had not mended from through all my years. Whatever the reason, it was the first time I realized that I had brought something into my personal life by designing the look and feel of the characters in a production. I had taken the experience and relationship of living with my father, a man who I viewed as deceitful at times and manipulating at most others. I put the look and feel of seeing his face and how his hair changed through the years into a cast that portrays people who are deceptive and manipulative of a system that decimated the Great American Pastime to a mingling of cheating and mistrust that took years to repair. Whether a metaphor or an epiphany, I found a therapeutic component of my craft that I have searched for in each script I read and every production I begin, careful not to cross the line between literal and figurative in my interpretation.

As I moved further away from my father, looking for something very different from what my mother and us children had to endure, I fell right into one of the most common societal tropes known to womankind. While I was hoping for someone as opposite as possible to my father, I married a man almost exactly like him. Charles Edward Clevering had that tan face and golden-brown ringlets perched upon his head and a raised lip smile that reminded me of my Paul Newman reverie when I met him working in a salon in Ft. Lauderdale. He was the son of staunch middle-class Irish Catholic parents, and his souped-up Chevy Impala called out to me, weakening my knees as it rolled up

---

THE MEDIA PURVEYS AN IDEAL ABOUT MALE AND FEMALE RELATIONSHIPS THAT IS LESS TANGIBLE THAN THE PAPER ON WHICH IT IS PRINTED.

---

the street and revved in front of my family's duplex. He was a hairstylist in the salon, and while he did his job well, after talking with him from time to time and watching him more often secretly in the mirror, I could tell that this would not be his career, his gaze drifting beyond the receptionist desk to the world that he felt was passing him by every moment he stayed inside the salon. His dreams and desires were solid and intoxicating to me, and we began to date. I look back on those days and nights going to the Elbow Room and dancing on the beach as a whirlwind of happiness, love at its infancy, and as the desire to be together incubated for more than a spring and summer; it was all but instinctual when he asked me to marry him that I confidently accepted. Hoping I had broken free from my past, I began a journey into the future, leaving my last name behind and taking a new one. The change of identity brought me a feeling of security and safety from the memories of men in my past.

Like many others in their early twenties, and especially in the 1960s, we found camaraderie in our struggles with the economy and the rigors of a new life together by entertaining friends with dinner and cocktails, the numbing flow of alcohol an invitation to open a little more to new acquaintances as well as each other, both personally and privately. Our move to California changed our tastes from rum and whiskey drinks adorned with fruit to the simple complexity of wines from Napa Valley and the occasional martini at a Hollywood hot spot. Regardless of the contents or shape of the glass, the drinks flowed freely, and the blur of beginning a new life began to take shape in memories I recalled all too well. As we struggled to make ends meet, my husband felt the burden of being "the man of the house" as his dreams and

Hugh Grant, *Nine Months*, 1995

aspirations unfurled more languidly, the changing breezes of the passing seasons ruffling his hopes that time was passing him by none for the better. The few drinks we had a week ago became the same consumed at night. The frustration he felt for his unrealized achievements began to materialize in the anger of his voice. His belligerent tone grew louder, seeking confrontation with each tip of the glass, the spike of alcohol fueling his fury to bait the response he so eagerly wanted to pull out of me. We began to argue more and more about less and less. As I thought marriage to this man would relinquish me of my subservience, instead, the alcohol, which had been a dominating theme with men of my past, was now seeping into my future, and I yearned for guidance from this path that I kept crossing.

The birth of our children, the move closer to family, and a better job for my husband all helped ease the pattern that had taken precedence in the early years of our marriage. Unfortunately, these replacements for his addiction were temporary, and the root of the problem persisted. His unhappiness with himself always seemed to shine more strongly with each sip of something, anything that was the flavor of the times, marked by a special on a blackboard on the wall at the local bar or whatever *Playboy Magazine* deemed the drink of the decade. Although he was never violent with me, I found myself retreating into the comfort of my children, knowing that I could find strength in protecting them from the man their father became when he drank. We consumed ourselves with sports, school activities, community service, and youth organizations. My decision to give up my goals in Hollywood paid off. After all, if I were on location, our children would turn out very differently, with only their father as their recognition of a role model or the lack thereof. When I began working again on movies, there were instances when one of my children would call, the phone ringing late at night, always conjuring horrors in my head of what might have happened with my husband or with him and my kids. Usually, it was how he had missed an event at school or not shown up to pick them up from their part-time job at the mall, only to be found home alone, the reek of alcohol verified by the bottle of booze lightly clenched in his hand dangling over the arm of the chair he had passed out in before the nightly news. I used to find excuses not to work on a film, whether it be the location, the hours, or the slight excess of money in the bank account that would justify staying at home to manage the situation, knowing from all the years of experience I had with my father that there was no cure to this affliction that never let go of my husband. I knew the one mistake my mother had made, and I had made it with my father and the men before my husband. I was unwilling to give up every piece of me, every desire I hoped for, and every dream I needed to realize. While I gave many of them away, a bargain for the sanctity of motherhood and marriage, once I could rekindle my career in the film business, I resolved to choose just that one thing for myself. It proved to be the only way I retained a resemblance to the strong woman that I had seen in my mind and had grown to become.

While I struggled to define myself at home, I could see the strength I spawned each time I left home to work on a film. Leaving behind an environment that defined the distinction between man and woman, husband and wife, and mother and father, I entered an androgynous realm where everyone was equal and necessary to make everything function properly. I had a job vital to everyone on the crew, and I had respect from men and women alike. I could express my opinions, and my creativity garnered genuine praise. There was happiness inside me, a self-satisfaction that didn't fear revelation amongst others, knowing it would be reciprocated rather than scorned as it was at home. I dreaded the day we wrapped a film. I had to return to my life as a wife with a husband who drank too much and loved too little, all while trying to retain some semblance of being a mother for my children to confide in.

Throughout all those years, the problems persisted, but there were always glimmers of the man I married and the wishes I wanted as a wife. The children grew and moved out from beneath our roof, leaving the two of us to face each other once again. This renewed commitment to one another and our return to Los Angeles helped invigorate happiness and acceptance in each of us. My husband began working in the film business again, and we often worked on the same movies together. Unknowingly, I found bringing him into my world of solitude to be a communal structure in which our relationship thrived. My control over those scenarios sifted into our marriage, and we found a middle ground where both of us found life meaningful. We found new hobbies and interests that we shared, such as antiquing in Pennsylvania. The memories we saw in the little shops sprinkled amidst the farmlands brought back stories of our childhoods, and I rediscovered my husband as if he was again revealing himself to me for the first time. Those years of our marriage, while we once again shared a similar career, were a return to the personal moments of our meeting in the salon, and his eyes again filled not with the glassed mask of alcohol but the expression of ambition to fulfill something more for me, the kids, and himself.

While life was beginning to present itself with hope and normalcy in the later years of our marriage, it was also preparing to do what life does best: bringing something our way that would shatter every hope we had. My husband had been working long hours on a film and shooting many

(Left Page to Right Page):
Dick Butkus, Jim Brown, *Any Given Sunday*, 1999

COACH'S LOCKER ROOM

nights in a row. As almost anyone in production will claim, it takes a toll on one's physical health when the body is deprived of sunlight because you are working through the night and trying to sleep when the world is wide awake. Our daughter had been married a few months before, and I threw that event into the mix as well when I noticed him becoming thinner and thinner, struggling to get out of bed from exhaustion, or so I thought. When our son called me from the hospital one Tuesday morning and let me know that he had checked his father in, I knew something was terribly wrong. Like most men, my husband would do everything possible to avoid going to the doctor, conjuring up miracle cures with over-the-counter medications to prevent a chest x-ray or the rubber glove. Over the next four days, I watched the man I had spent the majority of my life with dwindle into a mass of motionless flesh, tubes dripping with fluids for comfort more than nutrition. When the word "cancer" was finally uttered, I held on to my son, feeling his broad shoulders, a small reminder of his father's frame that was vanishing before my eyes. That Sunday morning, as soon as my son and I arrived at his hospital room, I heard the rattle in his breathing as I did with my father as he began to pass, and I knew what was happening before the blue light began to flash and the alarm rang out in the halls of intensive care.

We laid my husband and my children's father to rest that summer, and we each began to deal with the grief of losing someone with such a presence in our lives. Regardless of all the difficult times we had gone through, he was a family man first and foremost, and he loved us very much. While we each deal with grief in our own way, the suggestions of psychiatrists and acquaintances who had been through it before were without reprieve, and I resorted to the one thing that had helped me cope throughout the recent years to replace the loss that had been handed to me. Against the suggestions of all around me, I refused the pills and pillow talk, and I returned to work six months later. After all, it was the one place I had found strength before; the sense of community and camaraderie that filled a film set was my only medicine. Every morning, I looked at each date at the top of the call sheet as a countdown to my coping schedule, and it wasn't until I received the last piece of paper from the production assistant on the final day of filming that I realized what I had been given. After all the years of being a concubine to the shortcomings of the men in my life, I was finally free to discover the woman I am now. I could spend time alone without having to report to the men who selfishly confiscated my time, and through the sobs of sorrow, I began to wipe away tears of joy. I felt a sense of survival, and I began to explore all the passions and desires to live life on my terms, reflecting on the journey I had made and the obstacles I overcame, a strange fondness for those men who had made me the woman I am today. The only question in my mind was if there would be another, and that one was quickly answered over and over again.

As my career has put me in close contact with some of the most definitive leading male actors and heartthrobs of all time, my presumptions haven't risen much, so when I work with them, my expectations are exceeded. But then again, George Clooney and Brad Pitt are exceptional men way beyond their chiseled features and seductive smiles. My husband passed away twenty-seven years ago, and outside of a few first dates, I haven't had any other men in my life than those I work with on films. Having worked with many over and over and being years older than most, I have realized my role as a woman has changed from a woman who needs a man to a woman a man needs. I

George Clooney, *Out of Sight*, 1998

Brad Pitt, *Mr. & Mrs. Smith*, 2005

have discovered that during productions, when wives, girlfriends, grandmothers, and best friends are miles away, I have become the woman that each of them needs a replacement for in their life alone and away. Before you ask, no, I have not had any workplace romances. I am merely there to cook a meal for them, listen to their stories of past girlfriends, and let them complain about the lessons they won't repeat with future wives they haven't met yet.

I still have innocent crushes on a few male movie stars. Those infatuations are now more because of their talent, but that husky voice of Sam Elliot's and those Dr. Dreamy locks of wavy wonderfulness would make any woman swoon. Because I'm well beyond menopause, I can chuckle to myself when I see them walk across the set. I've come a long way from Paul Newman; I've loved a few people despite their flaws and am proud of the woman I have become.

I'M NOT AFRAID TO TALK ABOUT MYSELF TO ANYONE ANYMORE.

09

A DIRECTOR DIRECTS OTHERS TO DO SOMETHING THEY WOULD NOT USUALLY DO BY THEMSELVES.

It's something that is given, taken, mistaken, followed, misguided, and often communicated by someone who would have been better off just keeping their mouth shut: direction.

Fortunately, I have worked with some of the best at directing people, situations, emotions, motion, and the occasional non-human throughout my life, on and off a movie set. Whether it be an action scene, a romantic interlude, or a tantrum over the lack of butter on a table, the directors I have been in the presence of and seen working their craft have taught me more profound lessons than the movies we made. Each one of them has been unique in their approach, manner, and demeanor, all while orchestrating every name that rolls in the credits at the end of the film so that we achieve our common goal.

Before you even ask, no, I do not have a favorite. However, I've worked with some directors multiple times, deepening our professional relationships with each subsequent film and, in some cases, forming lifelong friendships. Some productions became what I would even refer to as a family affair. I was fortunate to work with John Hughes on *Curly Sue*. I witnessed his innate ability to convey nostalgia as we all bonded like brothers and sisters across every production department, feeling like a secondary cast character, albeit in the winter winds of Chicago. The freezing air whipping through the corridors along Michigan Avenue was stifled by the realization that we were contributing to an anthology of Mr. Hughes' films from the 1980s and '90s, which warmed our hearts and souls with tears and laughter. John had an uncanny ability to set the tone for actors and ensembles by simply calling out the word "Action." His voice, stern and abrupt, made that command sound like a father calling his son in from the front yard with the nervous anticipation of a lecture for something done wrong. Softer in volume, his voice made the exact same command sound like a close friend reassuring you that it's okay to cry on their shoulder. More than once, when John called out that single word, I almost moved my hand to make the sign of the cross, his voice echoing through the sound stage like the Pope saying "Amen" at the Vatican. The family affair with many of the same crew continued shortly after that. I was proud to be an attendant to Chris Columbus's graduation to director in *Nine Months*, where there was always an air of camaraderie. Hours did not matter in that movie as we witnessed the comic genius of Hugh Grant, Tom Arnold, and Robin Williams go off the rails all too many times. I found so much joy watching Mr. Columbus sit in his chair, eyes wide with astonishment at what those three lunatics would improvise, Chris only snapping out of his trance by finally remembering that they would have gone on for hours if he didn't call out, "Cut!" Those productions, which were too many to list here, were rewarded for all the dedication, hard work, and perseverance that seemed burdensome in other films.

And, yes, there are a few directors whose methods I may not have understood in the beginning, and under my

Jodie Foster, *Little Man Tate*, 1991

IT'S SOMETHING THAT IS GIVEN, TAKEN, MISTAKEN, FOLLOWED, MISGUIDED, AND OFTEN COMMUNICATED BY SOMEONE WHO WOULD HAVE BEEN BETTER OFF JUST KEEPING THEIR MOUTH SHUT: DIRECTION

---

breath, I mutter some not-so-pleasant sentiments privately and under my breath. But, even with those individuals, I developed an understanding of their intentions. In some regard, I joined their forces to deliver my best work at the bestowal of a madman or woman. Paul Verhoeven on Robocop always seemed to be directing the imagination as it was the first big-budget special effects film I worked on. Many of the elements seen in the final movie should have been present on the actual set. I had trouble, in the beginning, understanding the actors' choices for emotion and how explosions and gunfire were relevant when nothing was nearby. When I saw the first scenes in a viewing room near the production offices in Dallas, my jaw was unlocked from my face when fifteen-foot robot drones were destroying the set that a few weeks before looked poorly constructed to my naked eyes. This was also a similar experience to working with Christopher Nolan on *Insomnia*. Still, it was different in how Mr. Nolan made us all feel like we were seeing things that were not visible, much like Al Pacino in his leading role. Christopher had a unique ability to keep things in his mind: complex directions and commands for emotion that were only unveiled at the last minute, as we all questioned what was next and if what we were doing was relevant. This air of intrigue that Christopher Nolan created on set was a delight to see translate into the final edit, and it was a lesson learned for me that keeping on one's toes can lead to spontaneous moments of choreographed creativity.

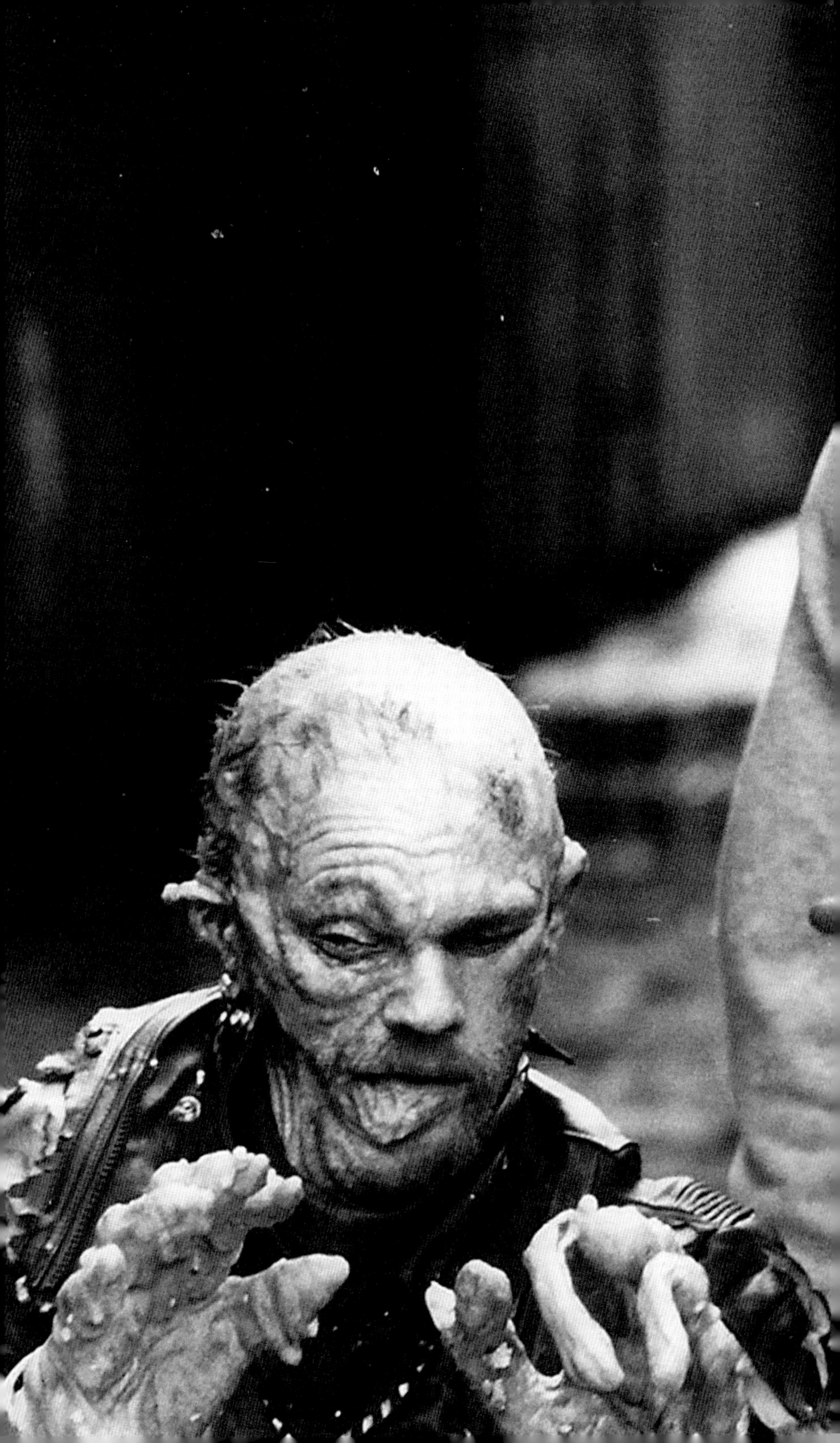

Paul Verhoeven and Peter Weller,
RoboCop, Pennsylvania Steel Mill, 1987

Speaking of choreography, nearly right out of the gate of going to work in Hollywood, I was treated to a front-row seat to see not only one of the great directors of the Golden Age of Hollywood but also one of the most outstanding performers to sashay across the silver screen. After seeing the choreography, costumes, and decisiveness of his lengthy film credits, I was introduced in person to the prowess and professionalism of a director by Gene Kelly on *Hello, Dolly!* His directing style was instructional from a place of compassion and gratitude. When he would perform dance moves as part of the choreography, there was never a moment of frustration if someone did not get the steps perfectly the first time. It was almost as if he recollected the development of his craft and conveyed to anyone in need the encouragement and confidence he had developed. Instead of stammering and stern commands, Mr. Kelly spoke softly and grinned, penetrating everyone's hearts, from millions of moviegoers to a single chorus line participant. Miraculously, they always performed to perfection on the very next take.

I learned watching Gene Kelly and Barbra Streisand communicate that an atmosphere of pleasantry is often a much more powerful motivator to success than instilling fear of failure in anyone not performing up to par. I took what I learned on that set and applied it to parenting, friendship, and colleagues. Of course, there are times and instances when a few stern words snap someone into place or an elevated tone while grounding my son for something he should have known better about instilled lessons that endured. Most of the time, I communicated with others with confidence in their abilities, creating empathy to navigate emotions and strength to go the extra mile. This was especially important when filming for what seemed like an eternity on nearly every Oliver Stone film I worked on for almost ten years of my life.

Oliver Stone, who I respectively and affectionately called "Ollie," was almost a hundred and eighty degrees away from the directing style of Gene Kelly. To say there is a method to Ollie's madness would insult his abilities. Perhaps his experience in Vietnam during the war led to his directing style or his desire to meander through chaos in search of serenity on the other side, a recollection of his tour of duty. Still, the reward for going into battle with Oliver Stone on the multiple movies I worked on was akin to a badge of honor. My first foray with Mr. Stone was *Born on the Fourth of July*, fittingly, a film backlit by the war that Ollie had seen from the front lines. I had not experienced a set run in an almost militant manner. His attention to every detail almost seems imperceivable. How one human can keep track of all the cameras, the lighting, the actors, the hundreds upon hundreds of extras, his sanity, and the crew was genuinely remarkable. There was such a necessity for authenticity that I had an actual military officer and United States Marine Barber oversee a haircut I gave to Tom Berenger, the exact method and each sweep of the clippers under absolute scrutiny. I feared that if I did not complete my task to regulation, I would have to drop and give that officer twenty pushups.

I first got my feet wet in that film because I had to attend to a platoon of extras in multiple scenes. In many films, a person considered "background" is put into costume, and their makeup and hair are quickly modified. This rapid attention to transforming someone who might not be an actor but is on set for a couple of meals and a measly paycheck is so that we can prepare hundreds of people for a crowd scene in which maybe only a few in the front row appear on camera. This was not the case with Oliver, ever. We put everyone through the "works"—wardrobe, makeup, hair, hand-laid facial hair, dirty hands, and props. Mr. Stone

Oliver Stone and Jim Brown, *Any Given Sunday*, 1999

wanted everyone to look as if they were present and could be captured on film at a moment's notice if one of them grabbed his perceptive vision. His attitude was that if one of us were to prepare for battle, all of us would be readied for war, charging toward victory and infamy.

This self-appointed "General of Cinema" did not emerge only for films with militant or military conflict as their subject matter. The next film I worked on with Ollie was equally regimented and disturbingly chaotic. In recollection, *JFK* was one of the more uncomfortable movies I worked on. You might think I would say that about *The Reaping* with Hilary Swank, where she is investigating biblical plagues, or *The Happening* with Zooey Deschanel, a film by M. Night Shyamalan, whose movies are known for being creepy. The difference was that I was in the middle of one of the most disturbing events many of us experienced in America. The characters and questions surrounding President Kennedy's assassination cast a haunting shadow over the entire set. Add the fact that we filmed in New Orleans, where everything seems soaked in voodoo, and I felt my shoulders around my ears every day I stepped on set. Oliver's attention to detail was so specific in this movie that there was even an anatomically correct, full-size replica of President Kennedy's nude body on the operating table of the Parkland Hospital operating room. It was a sight that caused me to gasp audibly every time I walked into that soundstage. Sprinkle the air of eeriness with Joe Pesci and his odd wig we created for the character of David Ferry, Tommy Lee Jones as Clay Shaw, who never broke character, and Kevin Costner, who took his role of Jim Garrison as seriously as the actual district attorney. There was very little reprieve from the weight that the event in 1962 shrouded upon our set. Walking through history as we filmed was fascinating. I developed pride in knowing that we were

Steven Soderbergh, *Ocean's Eleven*, 2001

Oliver Stone, *Any Given Sunday*, 1999

both questioning the narrative of history and capturing and delivering dignity to the man who left us that day in downtown Dallas. I am eternally grateful to Oliver Stone for believing in my abilities and skills.

The last film I did with Ollie was one of the most enjoyable and challenging. As a bonus, it was another sports film. Anyone who knows what a sports lunatic I am for anything with a scoreboard would understand how excited I was to be doing an Oliver Stone film about professional football titled *Any Given Sunday*. This would be the fourth film crew of Oliver's I would be a player in and the most ambitious in scale. Filming in Miami, where the Dolphins play, and Texas Stadium, home of the Cowboys, was a dream come true as I had only watched Sunday clashes from the stands. I stood on the fifty-yard lines of these hallowed cathedrals of sport with some iconic gladiators from football history. Jim Brown, Lawrence Taylor, and Terrell Owens were always so kind, almost protective of me, each day that it was hard to imagine their soft-spoken voices could shout taunts across the line as they squared off against other gridiron giants. Add to that the behemoths of cinema congregating in that cast of characters. Pacino, Heston, Ann Margaret, Quaid, Modine, and Cameron Diaz formed a team of talent that would have won a Super Bowl of acting prowess against almost any other film it squared off against. Oliver Stone assumed the role of captain, coach, and owner of the entire franchise, huddled in his video village of monitors for every camera, writing notes feverishly every down that was played, devising ways that he was going to be victorious over the struggles of production that arise on every film. Ollie has a way of creating chaos for the story's benefit and for the actors to draw emotions from. He allows it all to come screeching close to flying off the rails at any moment. Still, with this uncanny ability, he knows precisely when to pull back the reins and bring it all into the station unscathed.

Mr. Stone's obsession with authenticity, knowing how to return to normalcy on the other side of chaos, and instilling the belief that people can collectively conquer anything were some of the traits I learned from all those films, all lingering in my life as a friend, a mother, and a sibling. Oliver Stone taught me that never diverting from being authentic was a resounding method to preserving memories that last a lifetime rather than those built on false pretenses that vanish rapidly. No matter how difficult the subject or circumstances, my friend Ollie is one of the reasons why I am the person I am today in every aspect of my life.

When it comes to bringing a crew together like a family, no one does it better than the director I've worked with the most, Steven Soderbergh. If watching Oliver Stone is like observing a general overseeing the victory from afar, then Soderbergh is like a soldier charging in from the front line and running directly into the fire. Most directors are maestros at orchestrating a crew of hundreds regardless of each one's craft, from instructing actors, determining lighting, choreographing stunts, and even telling me if the hair is groomed for somebody running from an invisible alien threat. Generally, directors are precisely what their title implies: a director directs others to do something they would not usually do by themselves. So, when I first worked with Steven on *Out of Sight*, I was astonished at how being a "Director" defined him. To say he can do nearly every crew position on a set by himself would not be completely untrue. I have not seen him cook a meal or use a curling iron, but everything else is within his wheelhouse. After working with Jennifer Lopez and George Clooney to block the actions of the scene, he would help the cinematographer with lighting choices, give direct comments to everyone else with a boom microphone or prepping a prop before pulling the camera off a tripod, plastering his face to the

David Byrne, *True Stories*, Dallas, Texas, 1986

eyepiece, and softly commanding, “Action.” This approach allowed him to convey authentic visuals as if the audience was part of the scene, with slight movements to the frame and embedded angles rather than seeing the spectacle from a distance.

Steven directed one of the smoothest productions I ever worked on: *The Limey* with Terrence Stamp and the legendary Peter Fonda. It's not often that time flies on a set as dawn and dusk seem minutes rather than hours apart, but that film went like clockwork. Rarely does filmmaking seem like a nine-to-five job; however, I do remember multiple days on that short shoot that we filmed for less than twelve hours because we shot our entire list for the day. Being able to eat dinner when the rest of the West Coast was sitting down at a table was a real treat for those couple of months in 1998. Having completed two films with Steven

George Clooney and Julia Roberts,
***Confessions of a Dangerous Mind*, 2002**

at that point was all the preparation I would need to set forth on one of the most challenging and rewarding films in my nearly fifty years in production.

As I have explained earlier, *Erin Brockovich* was pivotal in my life and career, and it was one of the most anxious first days of production I have ever experienced, personally and professionally. Even after a few decades of doing what I did, I would always have butterflies at the beginning of a film, emotional anticipation for what might go wrong, and be pleasantly surprised when more went right than my mind imagined. If Steven had not commanded that film, knowing how calm he was and how he cared for everyone on set like family, I would have succumbed to panic attacks that rendered my hands useless. After all, I was about to work with arguably the most famous and revered set of locks in Hollywood at the time. As I sat in my trailer that

Tom Cruise and Frank Whaley,
***Born on the Fourth of July*, 1989**

first morning, waiting for Julia to arrive, an inaudible voice of doom built up in my head. It was quickly quieted when she came in and sat down in the chair. She was decisive yet listened when I shared, and the laughs we shared from early on in filming were warm auditory embraces that allowed me to gain more confidence in my craft than I'd felt for years. Shortly after our introduction to what would evolve into an extensive work relationship and life-long friendship, Steven walked into the trailer to see Julia and me deep in the creative process; his only comment was, "Looks like I walked into something really good here." And it was the beginning of something that I will dearly cherish for the remainder of my life, from day one to the final frame Julia and I filmed together.

This desire to create a climate of bonding continued in all the films that Steven directed, and I tried to provide legitimacy to the narrative and characters. I found this most necessary for the converging storylines and gritty characters of *Traffic*, our next film. From a continuity photo perspective, keeping up with the intersection of the characters in crisscrossing scenes was a challenge. There are times when Michael Douglas or Catherine Zeta-Jones' characters pass by Benicio Del Toro either in the foreground or background, and understanding where one or the other is in their respective narrative was necessary so that Steven was able to edit and assemble the final film in multiple ways to create the most tension in the audience. That was definitely one film I looked forward to finally seeing completed in the theater, as I was unaware of how everyone played out in each other's outcome from just being on the set. I was pleasantly surprised to see how each character's choices and the conclusion simultaneously affected each other.

I continued working with Steven as he jettisoned

the director role and instead executive produced two more films I was a part of: *Insomnia* and *Confessions of a Dangerous Mind*. Multiple crew positions were repeatedly filled by the same people on Steven's sets, so when we all migrated to the desert oasis of Las Vegas, we were primed and prepared for the most significant "family reunion" of them all: *Ocean's Eleven*. They say that spending more than three days in Vegas is too much, but the three months we spent in the Bellagio weren't nearly enough. They also claim that everything is bigger and better in Vegas, and this mantra was more than true with everything Julia, George, Don, Matt, Brad, and I did while working on that film. The pranks we played were more elaborate, the laughter louder, the conversations deeper, and the bonds more embedded in all our lives.

While I would go on to do two more movies with Steven, the *Ocean's* movies will always be the highlight of my time with Mr. Soderbergh. He instilled trust in me that I felt I had finally earned as an artist. The last film we worked on, *Full Frontal*, was so uniquely produced that no actor other than Julia was allowed to have someone present for their hair and makeup. Steven allowed me to participate in the production mostly because Julia wore a hair-lace wig, which was challenging to apply, but also because Steven realized my importance to the production. This respect I earned from Steven was something I took beyond the lights and cameras. It gave me confidence in my own life. I have traversed the grief of losing my husband, the uncertainty that I could provide for myself, and the realization that friends and family are truly the most important parts of anyone's life, giving them strength to accomplish and endure.

While Gene, Ollie, and Steven were the only ones I went

Julia Roberts, *Erin Brockovich*, 2000

2093

into detail about in this book, there was not a single director in my experiences in filmmaking that did not influence me, my craft, and my life in a unique and lasting way. After all, that is what they excel at—ensuring that everyone in a movie theater or in front of their TV experiences emotion and resonant imagery through their storytelling. Watching Jodie Foster and George Clooney venture from one side of the camera to behind the lens in their directorial debuts showed me what courage was at the cost of risking everything. These were the types of lessons and learning that I became accustomed to, and they were so much more than just being a hairstylist. Few people can say that their job has had such a positive impact on their personal life.

MY CAREER, IN MANY WAYS, DEFINED ME AS A PERSON BECAUSE OF WHOM I WITNESSED DIRECTING ALL THOSE MARVELOUS MOMENTS OF THE MOVIES I MADE.

10

THE SHOWER

Talk with any realtor, and they'll be the first to tell you that when someone tours a home, they generally have two complaints: the kitchen and the bathrooms.

Most people can get by with what the previous owner called a "kitchen." Ugly cabinets, old appliances, and a broken ice maker can easily be cured by food delivery and happy hours at a local bar. However, a house with a tiny shower or lousy lighting that makes makeup applications look more like *The Phantom of the Opera* than Rita Hayworth in Gilda can quickly turn what is considered a home into a new listing on the MLS.

During my decades of setting up temporary homes in production locations around the world, I always ensured the bathroom was the focal point of a hotel room or a rental property. After shooting next to icebergs in Alaska, the bed could be a little firmer than my aching back would require. A great caterer on set could replace the need to cook in a kitchen. And anything resembling a living room was only considered a place to style countless wigs for the next day's filming on mannequin heads that would have raised questions on whether I was a serial killer living next door.

I consider many items in my hairstyling arsenal to be tools. Curling irons, blow dryers, a myriad of combs and brushes, and enough styling products to resemble a Sephora on wheels are essential for creating some of the most memorable character tresses throughout my cinema history. I always giggled a bit when my many equipment cases would arrive at the production office at the beginning of a film. The crossed arms and shaking head of a line producer who just kept FedEx in business for another month with the money it cost to get all my "tools" to a remote location in Eastern Europe was sweet revenge for my having to fly economy to a film set with a two hundred-million-dollar budget.

After unpacking a seemingly endless number of styling tools into my trailer, I often looked at everything in more of a manner of a sorcerer than a stylist. Having an extended career in the movie business was much more than using my tools to create a particular "look." I had to look beyond the instructions on a blow dryer box or the suggested usage of a can of hair mousse to find new ways to assist talent in achieving thespian magic. I learned to manipulate the countless electrical devices and hair elixirs to extrude new usages that were more psychological than physical. The relaxing scent of lavender in a hairstyling gel on my hands, but not applied to the hair, was often enough to bring a calming effect to a tense scene.

While these styling tools have helped transform many actors into assassins or vampires, they are more than just something to curl or straighten hair. The warmth of a flat iron in the cold hours before dawn is sometimes more comforting than a cup of tea. The cold air button on a blow dryer in the steaming humidity of Louisiana rejuvenates anyone to do just one more take after an eighteen-hour

Hilary Swank, *P.S. I Love You*, 2007

THE SHOWER WAS MY SECRET WEAPON. WHAT LIES BEYOND THAT GLASS DOOR OR PERFECTLY RODDED CURTAIN BECAME THE MOST CRITICAL TOOL IN MY LIFE, PERSONALLY AND PROFESSIONALLY.

---

day of trudging through swamp lands amidst all manner of multi-legged creatures and some without legs at all. It's these inventive methods that differed me from the others, but it was these methods that were for someone else's benefit and not mine.

The one "tool" that I have found to be the most beneficial to me was not something in my trailer, but located in that one room I was so adamant about being special from the rest of the room or apartment I was sequestered to for months away from my actual home. The color of the walls, the lighting near the mirror, and the surface beneath my bare feet on days when they ached were all important in creating a zone of solitude and refreshment. I didn't feel like climbing up another flight of stairs in some old house in East Texas, but what lay beyond that glass door or perfectly ironed curtain became the most critical tool in my life, both personally and professionally. The shower was my secret weapon.

The sensation of water on the back of my neck, the aroma from my favorite conditioner, the soothing softness of bath gloves; the shower has always held a special place of memories, some good, and some that I bid farewell to as they were banished to the abyss beyond the drain between my feet. One of those memories in which I cherished the shower more than any other was also one that I wish I never experienced. My husband lay in bed dying of cancer, and I fought every tear back through strength and pain that I can only attribute to having gone through childbirth twice. Instead of letting him see the sorrow that was coursing through my veins, I saved my sobbing for the shower. He must have thought I had a severe hygiene disorder with the number of times he heard the water running in our bathroom. But knowing what he was going through and needing to be his last bit of strength, I shed every tear possible in there. Sometimes, the streams down my face accumulated in the basin more than what filtered from the faucet. Months after he passed, I continued to retreat when the tears would begin to swell, feeling a tiny bit closer to him now that he was gone, but also gaining strength to move on from the tragedy. Those memories are challenging to convey even in written words twenty-plus years later, so I'll leave them in the past.

A question I often get from someone interested in what I did as a career is commonly, "What was the most difficult production you worked on?" There is usually a long pause as I mentally run down my resume, stopping shortly at so many films that I am proud to have as credits, but also with pride that I even made it to the end. Some complex productions begin before the cameras even start rolling. Negotiating with a line producer on my contract can be equivalent to twelve rounds in the ring with Mike Tyson. My contract comprises several items I charge a production company for during the filming. There is my day rate when I am working on set and a different rate for idle days when I am stuck in a hotel in the middle of nowhere with nothing to do. As a union member, we also get overtime, double time, and triple time if filming for a day goes past twelve hours, which I never complained about because the money was good, and I was often sitting around getting paid because someone else couldn't figure out where to place

Jennifer Aniston, *Dumplin'*, 2018

a camera for the next scene. There is negotiating where I sit in the airplane on the way to and from my home to the location, shipping equipment, per diem for meals and other necessities, hair product budgets, wig rentals, hotel room type, or an apartment rent amount. These all sound like they should be standard amounts, but when a line producer calls me to go to work, the voice on the other end of the line always starts with, "Bonnie, we've got no money on this one." Movie of the week, independent projects, or massive budget franchises, the battle to get what I am worth after decades of doing what I do was always followed with an extended shower inhaling lavender from a conditioner bottle to calm my nerves.

After the amounts are agreed upon and the camera starts rolling, any number of people or instances can make production difficult. People are people; generally, they don't

Tim Allen, William H. Macy, Martin Lawrence, John Travolta, *Wild Hogs*, 2007

act like "Mommy Dearest" just because they think they can get away with it for the umpteenth time. Life is life, and when life gets in the way of one person on set, it can domino right down the line into the entire production. Thankfully, that doesn't often last, and the return to normalcy is usually a couple of call sheets away. Making a movie is stressful, and that's a massive understatement. I liken it to four years of high school in three months. Different aged individuals from various backgrounds coming together for a common purpose, navigating temperaments, emotions, differences of opinions, varied levels of ability, desires, and extracurricular activities all make graduating and moviemaking equally tricky tasks for a large group of people. If the head cheerleader breaks up with the quarterback on Thursday afternoon, those "Friday Night Lights" will not shine so bright for the rest of the team. I once overheard a producer saying to a journalist during an interview, "I prepare for the worst so that when it

Kristen Stewart, *Snow White and the Huntsman*, Great Britain, 2012

Kristen Stewart, *Snow White and the Huntsman*, Great Britain, 2012

happens, I know how to make the best of it." I do not listen to the voice of doom, but I have found it an excellent way to approach life daily. When production runs smoothly, it is like a speedboat cutting through the early morning glass-like lake. Scenes unfold effortlessly, hair changes are a breeze, and time flies by without friction. There is no single film like that, from fade-in to fade-out, but when it happens, even briefly, I can say my showers are much shorter.

It is not just people that can make a set akin to a raging sea squall. Locations can cause restless night sand vortexes of mayhem thanks to a few bottom feeders known as "paparazzi." That is why when I pause to answer the question of which production was the most difficult, it takes a moment to scroll down my IMDB page because that film is the second from last: *Snow White and the Huntsman*. I was fortunate to have Kristen Stewart, the producer, and long-time friend, Joe Roth, invite me to join them in and around London in the fall of 2011. It was with those two of my favorite people in the world, a phenomenal director, Rupert Sanders, and a group of makeup, wardrobe, and hair artists who were absolute professionals amid an evil queen and annoying dwarves, that made that production more tolerable while teetering on the verge of production hell.

So, how did this production transform from a fairytale to a numbing nightmare? Let us start with the location and home for nearly five months: London, England. If you have never been to what they call "The Capital," the best I can describe is a well-planned symphony where every instrument tries to play the same song in a different key. The massive melting pot of nearly every culture, language, and ideology in the same place simultaneously is enough to invoke a migraine by taking a single trip on the subway system. Getting used to not diving to the floorboard of a cab for the first few weeks as it turns onto what appears to be the wrong side of the street to us Americans is reason enough to command the cabbie to take me right back to Heathrow and the next flight out. Do not get me wrong; I love the culture, people, and shopping on Oxford Street. But coming from filming for fifteen hours where swords are slinging and screams are deafening, the last thing I want to do is hear a cacophony of car horns honking through the night.

The production company rented me a small flat in Kensington during those months in London. As always, I walked through several units in the building before settling on the one with the most inviting shower. The Everest green tile, brass fixtures, and dimmable recessed lighting were waiting every night when I retreated from the bustle of the city, but even more so from the sets and locations where we were filming. If you have not seen the movie, this dark twist on the Disney classic and characters takes place in a kingdom that has become a desolate wasteland of barren, twisting trees, bleak, snow-covered forests, and dingy castle walls. Maybe that is why they chose the infamous Pinewood Studios outside London that had been around since 1935 and served as the production nest for such film and television series as *Fiddler on the Roof*, *Superman*, *Alien*, *Teletubbies*, nearly every James Bond movie, and a couple hundred others that almost all of us have seen through the years. Pinewood is also a hop, skip, and jump from some of the most bleak and jagged terrain near any major European city. Carrying equipment through knee-deep water, ice-covered uneven rocks, and trying to stay warm in the wind chill that remains in your bones for days wears one down very quickly. And remember, we did this five days a week for nearly five months.

Hilary Swank, *P.S. I Love You*, 2007

I should have written an apology note to everyone in my apartment building for draining the hot water tanks nightly, but my shower needed to work overtime to prepare me for the next day. It was the intense shooting circumstances and the film's content. Much screaming, fighting, stunts, loud effects, and gray paint on everything, everywhere, took its mental toll on me and followed me to my shower. The water pressure was never enough to drown out the sounds of the day when the ringing in my ears of everything agitating would reverberate off those previously pleasant fixtures and inviting green tile. One of my favorite childhood Disney characters had invaded my sanctuary, and there was no hope of a happy ending.

During the same time we were filming, London became a little more difficult because of another movie I had worked on a year ago. Not only was Snow White in "The Capital," but Bella Swan was also there. *The Twilight Saga: Breaking Dawn - Part 1* was about to be released in theaters, and the publicity surrounding the story onscreen was exacerbated by the real-life love affair offscreen. I have been amid the paparazzi many times before and seen how life-altering their presence can be on myself, actors, friends, and family. Put a half-dozen of the biggest names from the last twenty years in the same hotel in Las Vegas to film *Ocean's Eleven*. Sin City's motto, "What happens in Vegas, stays in Vegas," is impossible to achieve as every meal, wager, and outfit is seen on every newsstand worldwide. The antics of the so-called photographers in London were exponentially worse. Fences were never high enough, curtains could not be drawn tighter, and chases on foot and car were worthy of any action sequence in a Schwarzenegger film. The mania around the movie matched the maniacal need to see Robert Pattinson and Kristen trying to get a cup of coffee, which was ridiculous in every sense of the word. Instead of being

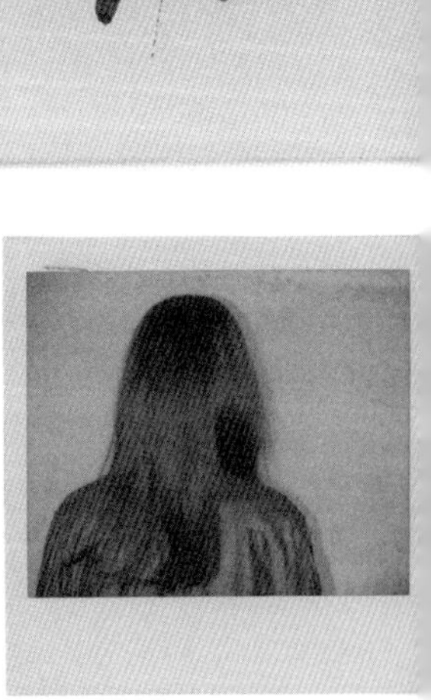

Julia Roberts, *America's Sweethearts*, 2001

Sc 93
NS
Restaurant
101
102
Eddie's
Suite
Kiss

able to enjoy restaurants and shopping, we sequestered ourselves in my tiny apartment because the photogs were planted deeply outside their residences. Cooking in the kitchen, a cocktail on the patio five floors from the ground, and watching old movies was our recluse. And my shower most nights was neglected until the morning when it was used and abused as just a way to wake me up or dampen the pang of a slight hangover from the dancing in the little living room away from the prying eyes of others.

Strangely enough, those nights hiding out with Kristen, Rob, and a few friends were some of my best memories while filming. The laughter in those walls away from eavesdropping journalists is probably the only way I made it through that production. My shower had been rendered relatively useless, and I vowed that would never happen again. Hence, the little voice in my head started repeating and rephrasing the sentence, "Maybe this is when I hang up my comb and shears." It was the first time I considered retirement. Walking through the challenging conditions in the English countryside was destroying the last fibers of tendons in my knees. Looking over my shoulder at who was following us was a constant pain in my neck. The weight on my shoulders of anxiety creeping up my spine with shrieks on set was reminding me every minute of every day that I was no longer capable of enduring the extreme physical and mental toll moviemaking takes on a person.

I remember a few showers in my life more than others. Every night after I got home from working with Faye Dunaway during what I call the "Mommy Dearest Episodes," finding out I had been voted into the Academy as the blasting water drowned out my screams of joy and the last shower I took in that flat in London. Knowing that I had made it to the end of that shooting schedule was a religious experience

Hilary Swank, *P.S. I Love You*, 2007

in my porcelain confessional, where I had cursed the world, prayed for strength, and promised impossibilities to the Lord, who I knew would forgive me if I came up a bit short on the number of Hail Mary's I never said because I was too tired from primping a princess to battle for her throne. As I closed the glass door for the final time, the echoes were silent, my skin moisturized with accomplishment, and the warm water helped ease the only pang, a slight hangover from the wrap party that I was happy to nurse into unemployment. That shower was a blissful moment of strength, re-energizing my desire to finish what I started and sitting silently away from the racket that had defiled the days before. One last turn of the hot and cold knobs and a fresh towel across my skin, I dressed in travel clothes, grabbed my carry-on, and climbed into a cab.

ONE MORE TRIP DOWN THE WRONG SIDE OF THE STREET, ONE MORE FILM UNDER MY BELT, AND A LITTLE BIT CLOSER TO WHAT WILL BE THE REST OF MY LIFE: RETIREMENT.

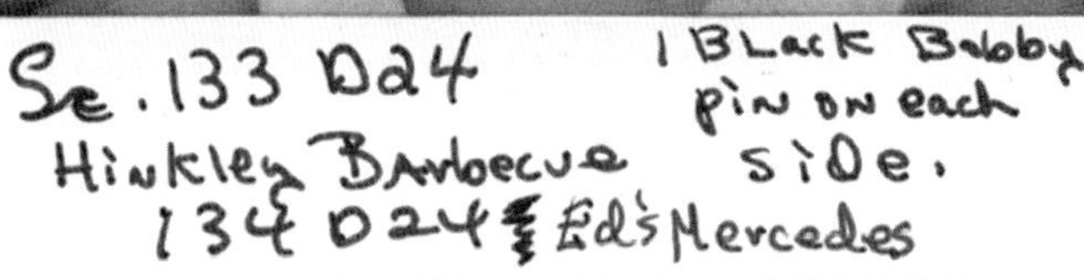

11

MEMORY BANK

AS IS TRUE IN LIFE,
MONEY CAN'T BUY
HAPPINESS,
AND IN HOLLYWOOD,
IT USUALLY BRINGS
ALONG SOME LEVEL
OF MISERY.

BEVERLY
HILLS

I vividly remember driving down Hollywood Boulevard at night for the first time. The neon lights flickered in a frantic rhythm as we drove by Grauman's Chinese Theater, Madame Tussaud's Wax Museum, and the countless souvenir shops and street performers, which constantly had me checking the side view mirror to see if Charlie Chaplin really did appear closer than he seemed.

The street reflected millions of colorful sparkling lights that lined the theaters and shops. This light parade is an infinite dance of tiny glimmers that shimmered in the headlights, giving the impression that if in the 1800s "them thar hills" were filled with gold, in 1964, the streets now were drizzled with diamonds. Dazzled by the beauty of that boulevard, I hung my hand out the window of our Pontiac, hoping to scoop up a handful of imaginary gems as we cruised down the street on our way to stake our claim in the "Valley of Dreams."

That night, my husband and I continued driving west toward the Pacific Ocean to watch the moonlight glisten on the cresting waves. Sitting on a cliff in Santa Monica where Tinsel Town's roar meets the Pacific waves' tranquility, we watched hippies gyrate around bonfires further down from surfers and bikini blondes wiggling to The Monkees. Having driven through America's version of Oz, our minds were filled with the wonderment that Southern California still possesses for all who reach its realm. As dawn's early light began to erase the stars above one by one, we finished our beers and let the ocean breeze push us gently back into the mundane morning of the San Fernando Valley.

Hand in hand with Hollywood's theme of two sides to everything, the truth be told, there is a reality and a fantasy to everything. During the warm, moon-filled night, we had traversed a land of glitz and glamour that only empires before had managed to equal. The fantasy was inspiring, riveting my senses and beckoning me like a sea siren guiding me to my new world. As we turned off Fairfax Avenue onto Hollywood Boulevard with the sun beginning to blaze on my bare neck, the reality shattered my smile, tarnishing the former buffet of brilliance with a strewn wasteland of discarded fliers for tourist attractions, bums scavenging trash cans, and the occasional hooker teetering on her crooked stilettos that had wobbled by Jimmy Stewart's star one too many times.

Hollywood's opulence in movies and magazines is a facade that enchants audiences and fame seekers to a reality that is more like Main Street at Disneyland. It gives the illusion of perfection and make-believe, but behind closed doors, there is nothing more than teenagers in cartoon costumes on cell phones standing next to their characters' furry heads. As is true in life, money can't buy happiness, and in Hollywood, it usually brings along some level of misery. To most of us, there never seems to be enough money, but when fame is added to the formula, money and misery seem to be exponentially exacerbated.

Brad Pitt, *Mr. & Mrs. Smith*, 2005

After living in a tiny apartment for years, my husband and I finally decided to rent a house. I had been working on bigger and bigger films and television shows, and our son had just been born. My husband had a good job, and while we weren't looking in neighborhoods named after women such as Beverly or Bel, two guys named Glen and Dale put together the perfect area of town for a beginning family. We moved into our small house at the foot of the hills. It didn't take fancy furniture or Persian rugs to make it a home; I just needed to fill those four walls with a fragrant scent that reminded me of people and places from my past that seemingly permeated the air from Malibu to Palm Springs.

Years before, my family and I lived in a small house in Aurora, Illinois, not on the other side of the tracks, but close enough to attend school at West Aurora High with the

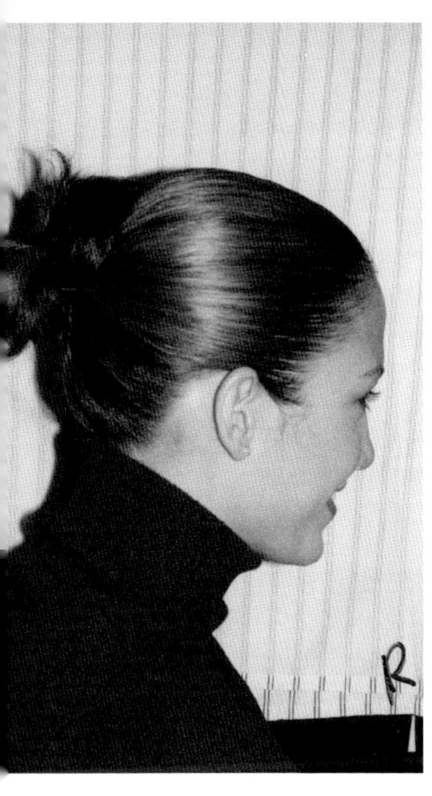

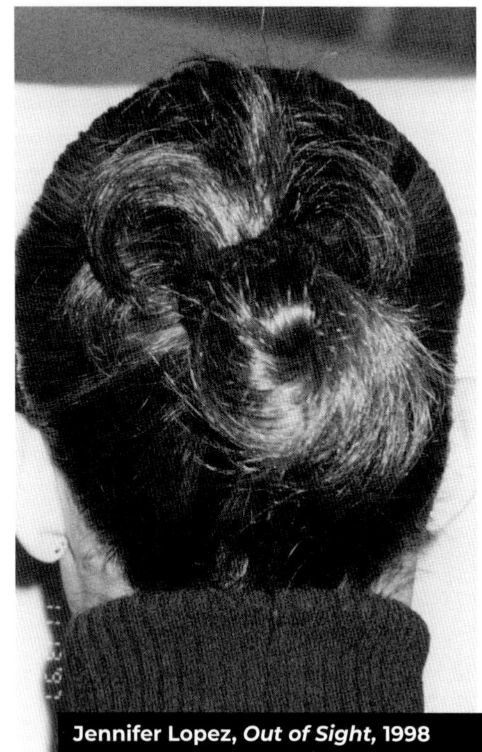

Jennifer Lopez, *Out of Sight*, 1998

more fortunate kids. There, I met my first boyfriend, Johnny Goodfellow, the son of a doctor destined to follow in his father's footsteps with a divine last name. Johnny and his family lived just outside town in a large home with horses and hounds that wandered the stately property, contrasting with the working-class neighborhood that consumed most of the city. Looking back, Johnny was handsome, dressed nicely, and wore cologne when most boys smelled like a locker room. Sitting with him on the overstuffed leather sofa in his parents' living room comforted me. Still, the smell of the surroundings made me swoon as the night dew tufted on the moonlit breeze, drifting in through the open bay windows, filling every deep breath I released with a sigh. I sat there dreaming of one day having a home filled with Ethan Allen furniture and gold-trimmed Limoges plates filling the buffet cabinet next to the twelve-person dining

"QUIET QUALITY" HAS BEEN MY MANTRA FOR MY ENTIRE LIFE. THAT IS WHY I AM HAPPY WITH MY NAME APPEARING AT THE END OF A MOVIE RATHER THAN AT THE BEGINNING.

---

table that reflected the Starscape of the chandelier above it in the perfectly polished mahogany. Although everything that represented wealth was presented around me those nights, only one element made me feel encompassed in the comforts of luxury. The single floral scent sat in dried bunches of seeds in the living room and the bathrooms in wicker baskets and little glass bowls, color-coordinated with drapes and hand towels. Although the sunlight had faded its deep purple into a grayish blue, the smell of lavender is the only fond memory of Johnny Goodfellow I recall today.

Lavender is my earliest recollection of what I comprehended as wealth. While growing up in Aurora, I spent a lot of time in my parents' small grocery store. The smell of fresh meats and spilled milk in that mini-market were polar opposites to the rich floral notes of lavender perfume worn by women who paid with bills rather than coins. Now, driving past the palm tree-lined streets of Beverly Hills, I felt I was inhaling lavender in the oxygen around me. I could only imagine the smell inside those enormous mansions, where I equated the purity of the scent to the number of square feet, and I nearly hyperventilated trying to breathe it all in.

However, no matter how intoxicating the smell of money and success, I could always think back to my upbringing and remember one of the most important lessons of my youth, which equally applied to the fundamentals of Hollywood:

never lose perspective. This is a lesson everyone in the film business has had to learn to keep from becoming page one of a paparazzo's portfolio.

Defining what constitutes luxury and necessity is crucial to have a frame of reference. One of the earliest lessons I learned was from Julia Roberts on the set of our first film together, *Erin Brockovich*. Before I got the job, I remember getting a call from Julia's manager asking if I was the hair stylist who did Jennifer Lopez's hair in *Out of Sight* and that Julia was interested in meeting me. A few weeks later, we were working together. We spent four months in Barstow and Ojai, California; both were in opposite directions from Rodeo Drive but equally as Walmart from their Gucci counterpart. She played her famous character, which was as different from her real life as any role she had ever played. Over that time, I realized that she was every bit of Erin Brockovich in reality, minus the push-up bras and teased multi-colored hair. One instance that always makes me laugh is how one of the most famous women in cinema history never lost perspective on what happened throughout the film.

Here I was, working with an acting icon—someone who had been relatively financially stable throughout her entire existence on Earth. She could afford everything on Rodeo Drive, in any store, driving any car a valet could park, and with everyone catering to her every need. As we finished filming, I sat on the set one day and started making my list of upcoming Christmas presents for family and friends. My list consisted of Starbucks gift cards and antique pillowcases. I leaned over to Julia and asked her if she had many gifts to buy.

She replied, "No."

I was shocked. She seemed generous with those around her and by no means lavish with anyone, but she must have a list of friends and family who deserved luxuries from all the fanciest boutiques.

Julia said, “I think we should make gifts for people this year.”

That afternoon, we stopped by a knitting store in the little town where we were staying, and my education in the world of stocking stitches and purls was about to begin with Professor Julia Fiona Roberts, who was the head of the class.

Every time the director yelled, “Cut!” for the next few months, it was a vocal starting pistol for our arts and crafts marathon. Bundles of colored yarn, knitting, and crochet needles appeared from concealed pockets in jackets and bags, leaving the security guards scratching their heads, wondering what else somebody could have brought onto the closed set. Our hands were a blinding blur of movement for the next few minutes as we knitted scarves for some and crocheted other items for others. While Julia and the others were highly skilled, my ambition got the best of me when I attempted a shawl that the crew suggested I donate as a decorative net to the seafood restaurant opening down the road. Over the years, I have picked up some yarn and a new set of needles as if the latest material they are made of would empower my skills differently. However, I still struggle, but with much laughter, remembering those days sitting with Julia Roberts in her *Erin Brockovich* wardrobe, as far away from Rodeo Drive as our hearts and minds could be.

As I have moved through my life and career, I have seen opulence magnified with each more elaborate production that movie minds can dream up. It has become clearer to me

Julia Roberts, *Erin Brockovich*, 2000

Nancy McKeon and Michael J. Fox, *Poison Ivy*, 1985

how little it all means. The most expensive movie, with the most prominent actors and the most special effects, won't always tell a great story. The illusion is that the more money, the greater the story when the opposite is true. Our lives are defined by our stories, memories, moments of laughter and tears, and how we overcome our own odds. The single mother who holds two jobs and cares for her three children while revealing the atrocities of a global conglomerate is much more compelling than a married couple of assassins who try to kill each other. Most people in ten years won't remember Steve Jobs because of his wealth, but rather his contribution to ingenuity and innovation. In this era of opulence that we live in, trading one credit card for another, I have found the easiest path in life and through Hollywood to be the quiet side streets rather than the boisterous avenues. "Quiet quality" has been my mantra for my entire life. That is why I am happy with my name appearing at the end of a movie rather than at the beginning. I define my life and career with sincerity toward stories and relationships rather than headlines and scandals.

Sure, I have moments of wanting the newest handbag and the piece of jewelry in the boutique that I pass each day on my way to the grocery store, stopping with my nose nearly pressing the glass in wide-eyed adoration. I do my fair share of supporting the global economy and tax structure with purchases, but always within reason and never for the sake of trying to improve my sense of wealth with material goods. I can look back at all my possessions in life and retell the story of why I have that item, and with each memory, I define my life in my own way, adding up to the sum of who I am, where I have been, and what I have accomplished.

Although it may seem the contrary, I am not against spending money. After all, we don't work eighteen-hour days on the tundra at the foot of a glacier in Alaska during the filming of the movie *Insomnia* just to pay utility bills and student loans. When you spend money, what's most important is that the item holds significance, regardless of what it is or its monetary value. When giving a gift, it feels good to know that the recipient will appreciate the thought behind it rather than see it as a display of wealth. Elvis didn't rent out Disneyland for twenty people in his group to prove his wealth. He did it to find normalcy in his wealth and fame and to share it with the people in his life who would appreciate the gesture and his quest. Years ago, I remember a colleague of mine and a friend of George Clooney's telling me about the Christmas present George had given to a few of his close circle of guy friends. George had personally delivered an expensive motorcycle to each of their houses. Having known George Clooney for years, I knew exactly why he gave those gifts. Anyone else who read the story in the tabloids must have thought what an arrogant and ostentatious movie star he must be to spend money on people like that, but the opposite couldn't be more accurate. He knew each of those guys for years, and the gift was a way to bring them together, allowing them to do something as a group that was liberating while letting them escape from the doldrums and pressures of Hollywood.

Even though the memorable moments of Hollywood of late have been more in courtrooms than cinemas, the lasting memories we, as production people, make in movies are not for the sole purpose of ticket sales and golden award statues. While a series of box office flops will put the skids on a burgeoning career of the best of talents, one of the main reasons that people like me do what we do for a living is to make memories for ourselves and for the ability to touch the lives of those who see our work. And while most of us get paid relatively well, working the hours we work in the conditions that we endure, there are many other ways to make a lot more money without the relationship risks that a four-month production can put on even the strongest and longest marriages. The wealth we generate is in those times of laughter, tears, struggles, and accomplishments. The ability to knit a fishing net of a scarf with a future Academy Award winner on a little film with no special effects that told a story about rags to riches and going from insignificant to insurmountable through determination and persistence is what I will be remembered for, more than the wealth that I have attained.

While I have been fortunate to have made many films and amassed a gold mine of memories, the houses and cars, handbags, and necklaces that are the material embodiment of those memories ultimately take me back to a moment many years ago.

After leaving the studio on Friday evening, I had to make one stop before I spent the weekend finishing unpacking the moving boxes in our first house. That Saturday morning, after I unpacked the mismatched dishes and the hand towels that we had snuck out of motels we stayed in on our cross-country drive, I opened the small bag that held my purchase from the day before and cradled in my hand the netted pouch tied with a pastel ribbon. The smell of lavender seeped through the tiny holes in the taffeta bag, and my mind was filled with memories. I walked around the house, letting the scent of lavender cover everything inside, and I sat on the window seat, looking out at the other houses across the street.

SMILING, I KNEW THEN THAT OURS WAS NOT THE LARGEST, BUT IT WAS THE WEALTHIEST, AND IT HAD BECOME OUR HOME, PRICELESS IN THE MEMORIES WE WOULD MAKE INSIDE AND OUTSIDE ITS WALLS.

Black Thick Pony Tail BAND

Sc180 D33
PASSES out in PARKing LOT
6/22/98

12
WITHOUT HONORS

I never really cared for attention. There was never a starring role in a school play or a tryout for cheerleaders. I left that up to my sisters or those who really wanted it, or at least their parents, who convinced themselves of a need to apply makeup for all the attention they missed as kids. I've appeared in a few movies, playing cards at a table in *Leaves of Grass* and sticking an earring in Hugh Grant's ear before running away when he shrieks in *Nine Months.* I offered "Coffee, Tea, or Me" to Al Pacino on an airplane scene in *Any Given Sunday*, but I've never asked for any of these roles. They have always been for fun because someone dared me to, or they forgot to cast talent while I was standing there on the set, talking on my cell phone and just happened to catch Oliver Stone's eye. I've found the limelight to be stark white, failing to flatter me in a golden glow, a bank of fluorescent tubes glaring down, causing me to cower in the corner, posturing away from popularity.

No one enjoys being scrutinized, and the movie industry is built on instinctively rejecting anything that may challenge the status quo or expose problems within the system. Those seeking stardom often face this scrutiny the most. I have an unbridled respect for actors and their craft, not always on set, but eternally before they are camera-

I'VE FOUND THE LIMELIGHT TO BE STARK WHITE, FAILING TO FLATTER ME IN A GOLDEN GLOW, A BANK OF FLUORESCENT TUBES GLARING DOWN, CAUSING ME TO COWER IN THE CORNER, POSTURING AWAY FROM POPULARITY.

---

ready. I would rather have another hysterectomy than be subject to the brutality of casting agents that actors see every day of their careers. They stand on command like a specimen placed under microscopic inspection, meticulously dissected by a seated group of people hiding behind a folding table, collectively determining an actor's fate by the inflections in their voice, the ability to command two tears rather than three, and whether that extra California roll the night before is showing in swollen ankles. Actors often consider the words "We'll give you a call" like playing Russian roulette. After experiencing a lot of rejection and verbal abuse, actors develop a tough exterior to protect themselves from the emotional toll of hearing that phrase, which is essentially a death sentence for their hopes of getting a role. I'd rather be vulnerable to the rigors of life than subject to another person's determination of the outcome of my destiny.

Although I fear scrutiny, I take criticism fairly well, better than most. Perhaps it's that I'd rather keep my mouth shut than have somebody with thinner skin feel penetrated by my retort. I recoil from the kill, knowing it's safer for me to choose a different path than trudge forward into a melee of he said, she said. In the end, I ask myself, "Is it worth the fight?" when someone I know is incompetent tries to assert themselves beyond their capabilities. I wait silently, foreseeing the future for a moment when I can chuckle to

***The Twilight Saga* (2009 - 2012)**

myself as they fall flat on their face, finally realizing they are in way over their head, watching the culmination of the metaphorical train wreck. Over time, I have learned and developed two rules when it comes to criticism: "If you are going to dish it out, you better be able to take it," and "Make sure you know what the heck you are talking about before you preach to the choir." The latter is always more unforgiving. People gallantly walk away from failed criticism and talk to everyone within earshot of your dereliction, like a gaggle of old hens in their Sunday best with nothing better to do than make themselves feel a little bit better by dragging your character downhill through the slop and mud. Hollywood is at the bottom of a hillside, and a little criticism goes a long way down.

On average, only about ten percent of movies profit each year. Of those, the top two percent of profitable films offset the entire remainder of losses in the industry. Even with the advent of subscription networks and more outlets for movies and series, honors in the entertainment business are few and far between, generally gauged by ticket sales and the data from home market viewings via the latest technology device. As I have mentioned before, the process of creating a film, from the initial idea to its distribution, is a remarkable achievement. Despite spending countless hours away from family and friends, dedicating our lives to creating entertainment for the masses, I find great honor in having my name listed in the credits at the end of a movie. I've been honored over 100 times in my career, and each time is as appreciated as the last. The size of the honor is no different, whether it be a movie of the week or a major motion picture. I take great pride in my work and don't seek recognition for it. The honor I'm most proud of is being invited to be part of something representing the pinnacle of achievement in film history.

The honor bestowed upon me 23 years ago receives little recognition except for one night a year. On this night, hundreds of millions of people realize the recognition I have received when asked to express my expertise in the industry where I practice my craft. Although this honor is personified by a few people publicly, the importance of this responsibility that I have been given is equal amongst all of us who have been included in this club of sorts for nearly a century. I am only one of less than eleven thousand people in the world who have been invited to make decisions on the industry's future and, in some instances, determine the outlook of talent's critical acceptance for the foreseeable future. Thanks to Joe Roth and Julia Roberts, who signed my application and nominated me over a decade ago, I became a Motion Picture Academy of Arts and Sciences member, always known as the ones who voted at the Oscars.

When I received my Academy card in the mail, along with my acceptance letter (now beautifully framed and hanging on my wall), I felt verified in my expertise and dedication to my craft. It represented decades of career development and the body of work that had entertained audiences for years. I was included among my peers, those still with us, and those who had passed on, and I also felt something more personal. This was not an honor for a particular movie or hairstyle that I had created, and it was more than just inclusion among others who were capable of far more than I had achieved and who had impacted the industry and society in more significant ways than my contributions to cinema. I had received recognition for my decisions in life to become more than just a hairstylist. I was rewarded and recognized for my contributions as a daughter, sister, wife, mother, and friend to a select few. I gained this recognition by defining my life, persona, spirit, and influence through movies and those who shared them

Kristen Stewart, *Snow White and the Huntsman*,
Marloes Sands Beach, United Kingdom, 2011

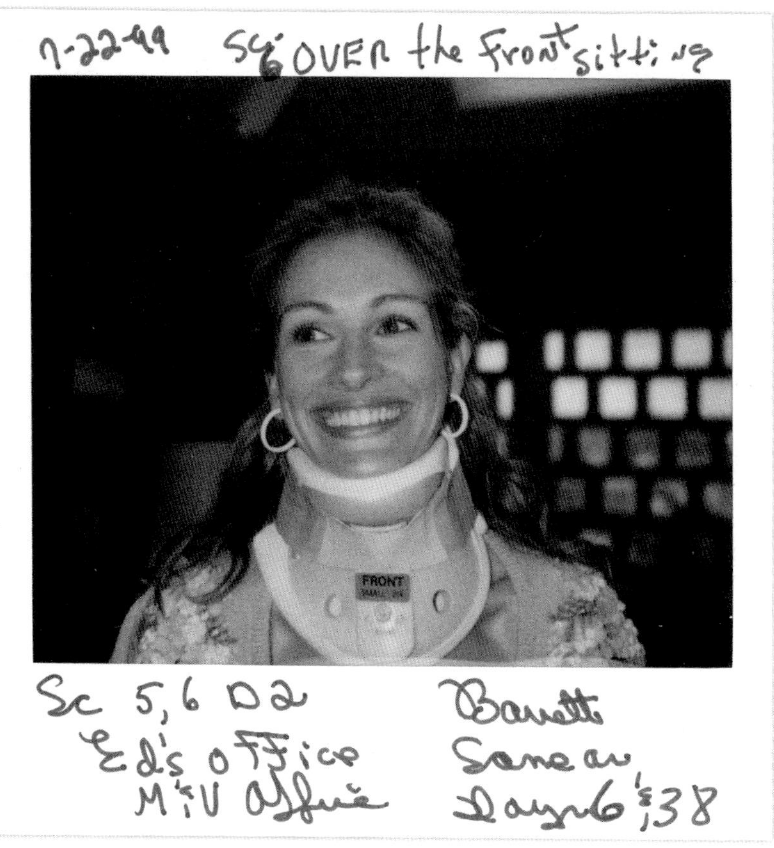

Julia Roberts, *Erin Brockovich*, 2000

with me. Each time I pass the framed acceptance certificate on the wall in the hall or show my membership card at the movie theater to get in for free, I pause to realize what it all means. It means that I have achieved a status in life and in my career without seeking it, but I have been recognized by audiences, viewers, my children, and my close friends as someone content with her life. That is the most incredible honor anyone can have.

Being a member of the Academy has taught me a lot

about determining who receives an award and how they should be honored. I watch hundreds of films each year: the rare choice that makes my all-time best list, many that are good, and some I appreciate for the effort in completing the process of creating a film. After watching countless films over the years, I always have trouble recalling the past year's Oscar winners, partly due to my age. Just when I forget, I'm reminded of the tradition where last year's best actor and actress winners present the awards to the current year's recipients. It's not as if I don't care who won it last or how many they took home. Still, I wouldn't say I like seeing someone set to fall from the grace that is bestowed on them. The awards stage is more of a shooting gallery for the critics who can't wait to take their best shot, knocking the talented individual, team, or group from their pedestal and extinguishing the spotlight with the reviews of their

I'D RATHER BE VULNERABLE TO THE RIGORS OF LIFE THAN SUBJECT TO ANOTHER PERSON'S DETERMINATION OF THE OUTCOME OF MY DESTINY.

next film. As the television cameras pan around the crowd to show the nominees who didn't win clapping for the victor, I can't help but try to read their minds, the thought that a bullet had been dodged, leaving them open to doing their best once again on another project, their minds clear from the pressure that they have to live up to the legacy of themselves through a statue that sits on their mantle or travels from hotel room to hotel room with them on each subsequent film. While the honors are welcomed as verification of achievement, some rewards occur on set each day, which has always struck me with a more lasting significance of satisfaction in fulfillment of personal honor.

Hilary Swank, *The Reaping*, 2007

Those insignificant moments in the life of a film crew member impact the industry without physical reward. This had occurred many times in my tenure from M. Knight Shyamalan, who donated a vacation getaway to one crew member when it came to Dollar Day each week on *The Happening* so that someone could enjoy a moment with a friend or loved one whom he had taken away for months to help realize his dream. I've been a precise part of spending days and nights baking over a thousand Christmas cookies with Kristen Stewart so that an entire crew on *The Twilight Saga: Breaking Dawn* could understand how much they meant to her personally as she embraced their dedication to making her performance the best that she could deliver. These impartial gestures of gratitude from individuals who can afford to limit their emotional access to almost anyone remind me of the honor I have received working with them to make a piece of history no matter what the box office takes at the end of opening weekend.

These gestures of honoring others bring a crew together, rallying them behind a cause and carrying the weak and weary through the long hours of production and the months of solitude from loved ones. These are the kinds of honors that I strive to embody in my personal life outside of my work. It's an honor for me to be able to positively impact someone's life by simply acknowledging their abilities, no matter how small they may seem. Whether it is a special meal for my family to let them know how much I appreciated them cleaning the yard and tidying their rooms or the rhubarb pie I delivered to the priest after mass to let him know how much his sermon meant and as a notification that I was listening when he spoke to us in the congregation. These are the awards I have learned to graciously hand out year after year from my lessons learned on the film set and as a member of the Academy.

While I have never given an acceptance speech for an award, I always look forward to hearing from the winners in each category, clinging to every praise they give to someone involved in their achievement, applauding those that I know for being recognized by the recipient personally, in their way, even without the golden statue as validation. I've practiced my speeches in various tones, rehearsing the inflections in my voice and the gestures with my hands, eyes focused with honesty. However, these speeches are typically intended for a single person or a small private group. I have learned how to deliver a speech from some of the best. The way she holds hands gently but with a firmness of sincerity each time Hilary Swank tells me how much my work has meant to her when we finish a film, the sincerity of her as a person, noticing the emotions in her eyes as she expresses the value of our friendship.

I have taken what I have learned and delivered speeches at parent-teacher conferences when I know one of the kids has made their job difficult. I have placed my hand on the back of someone dear to me to encourage them when they have finally stood firm and decided to end a love affair lacking the critical ingredient of love. These speeches are simple and concise, and while they are not meant to rally a cause or change the universe, the simple act of encouragement can mean a lot to someone who gets little recognition for their efforts and, in turn, can begin to affect their outlook on themselves and their future, inspiring them to do things with their life, no matter how minimal, that can bring change to themselves and those around them. The recognition of the meaning and intent of my speech in a smile, a tear of

Kristen Stewart, *Snow White and the Huntsman*, 2012

exhalation, or a stiff upper lip, and a nod of a head means that my speech has hit home with my audience, and that's when I sit back and enjoy watching someone refine and motivate themselves and others.

Unfortunately, each year, a segment of the Oscar telecast recognizes those who have passed away each year in memoriam. There are usually never enough movies to showcase their talent and not nearly enough time to share in their lives. As I grow older, the names and pictures that appear become more familiar and in number. I have lost friends and mentors; for many of them, this is the first and last time the general public has been made aware of who they are and what they have achieved. As many of these people were my superiors in rank and talent, I remember the speeches they gave me, words of encouragement that helped me do my job better or strive to make a difference in my life. Some speeches comforted me in times of despair, and others pushed my limits when the last thing I wanted to do was another extra's hair in the freezing cold hours of the morning. The voices of my beloved ones who have passed still echo in my ears to this day, all sharing a resounding common theme: as much as I would like another day with them, no more words are necessary to complete our time together or strengthen our relationship. These speeches and honoring those we respect and care for are the most impactful and essential to deliver each day of our lives, as our time together can be interrupted at less than a moment's notice. I look back on relationships with those who have passed and regret not summing up and concluding things I wanted to say to certain people. But, for the majority, I am at peace with those in my life, letting them know my concerns or appreciation so that our relationships are complete each day. While there may sometimes be struggles between siblings or parents or in the way a friend responded when you wanted them to confirm the contrary, the need to deliver speeches and honor the relationship, especially when there is a disagreement over minor issues, is important in order to resolve it and to prevent any feelings of regret when it's too late.

As I get closer and closer to joining those "In Memoriam" for those Academy members who have passed during the year, I look at my life and career and try to authenticate to myself if I deserve to be counted among those who receive statues each year at the Oscars. I conclude that authentication isn't about a single award, but rather completing a daily checklist of living life to its fullest, not just for myself but for those in my life who mean so much to me. This selfless attitude and approach to living gives me satisfaction that I hope instills honor in those who share my life. As a motion picture hairstylist, I look at the

Tom Cruise and Frank Whaley,
***Born on the Fourth of July*, 1989**

Robert Pattinson and Kristen Stewart, *Twilight: Eclipse*, 2010

Julia Roberts and I a few hours after she won the Oscar, L'Ermitage, Beverly Hills, California, 2001

Horton Foote with his Oscar for *Tender Mercies* on the set of the film *1918*, 1985

honor in my career as the ability to deliver emotion and experience to the actors and characters that audiences respond to each time they sit through one of the films I have worked on, without the care of being recognized publicly for my work. Regardless of award and merit, the honor has been the same as the first time I stepped on set and began to live a dream of doing what I do. As a human being, I have been honored with the awareness of my growth, experiences, and accomplishments as a woman who has loved a few and cared for many unselfishly.

AND, AS MUCH AS I WOULD BE HONORED BY A STATUE FOR MY ACHIEVEMENTS IN FILM, THE DAILY REWARDS OF BEING WHO I AM, EXACTLY AS I WANT TO BE, WITHOUT REMORSE OR NEED TO SAY ONE MORE WORD TO ANYONE, IS THE LIFETIME ACHIEVEMENT AWARD I HAVE GIVEN MYSELF TIME AND TIME AGAIN, LOOKING IN THE MIRROR, RIGHT AFTER I HAVE REHEARSED MY OSCAR SPEECH FOR THE THOUSANDTH TIME.

13 INTO THE SUNSET

**MOST OF MY ADMIRATION
FOR PEOPLE IN MY LIFE
IS NOT WHAT THEY HAVE
ACHIEVED WITH AN OSCAR,
EMMY, OR GRAMMY,
BUT HOW THEY BROUGHT
CONTINUITY OF LIFE BACK
INTO BALANCE AT
THE CENTER OF THE INFINITE
LOOP MORE OFTEN
AND WITH GREATER EASE.**

More than a few times while on set, I stood in complete awe, my proverbial jaw hitting the floor, unable to move, as I witnessed incredible scenes unfold before my eyes. It's more than witnessing a man land on the moon or when the love of your life enters the room for the first time. Some moments are priceless but can't compare to what I have seen on set. Gene Kelly directed a hundred chorus girls in perfect syncopated movement on the *Hello, Dolly!* set, a vision of beauty undefined by color and sound. The intricacies of the cables, pistons, and other electronic components that made the mechanical reindeer fly while Tim Allen sat atop as "Santa Claus" were so complex that only NASA could truly understand them. Their engineering brilliance was as awe-inspiring as a child's first sight of presents under the Christmas tree, supposedly left by the bearded man himself. Julia Roberts sashaying down the staircase in her red suit on *Ocean's Eleven* was grace, beauty, and sophistication that only princesses in fairy tales possess.

The top prize for jaw-dropping moments is the first big-budget action movie I worked on in 1984. The crew had heard the ideas, the production designer shared sketches, and the Art Director shuffled through samples of materials

I HAD THE PERFECT ENDING TO COUNTLESS SCENES OF A LIFE THAT FOUND CONTINUITY IN EVERY ASPECT.

that looked as if they had been part of the UFO recovery at Roswell. But nothing could have prepared me or my agape mouth for when Peter Weller first stepped on the set in full costume on *Robocop*. He was huge, the studio lights bouncing off his metallic helmet mesmerized me, and I couldn't help but swoon with each thud of his oversized boots that shook the set around me. Even with all the sound effects and orchestral score, the film itself couldn't replicate the impression of seeing it all in person. The sensation of that sight still lingers in my memory thirty years later, but unfortunately, my recollection was starting to manifest in my body, and I was starting to feel like Robocop looked that day in Dallas.

After more or less a few million repetitions of pulling hair with a round brush, holding an exhaustive blow dryer for a cumulative couple of years, and marching up inclines to ensure a hair-lace wig looked perfect on the soon-to-be victim of a fang-wielding Robert Pattinson, my body was starting to fall apart, in need of the same mechanical parts that Robocop was made from in that film of the same name. A partial knee replacement, shoulder surgery, shoulder replacement, and the possibility of another knee being reconstructed; I felt like what all those players in *Any Given Sunday* and *Friday Night Lights* looked like after I sent them onto the set and slamming into each other on the screen. Moviemaking is a physical experience, not just the action but the toll the process takes on your mind and body. With every creak of my joints, I started to heed that little voice imploring me to start acting my age. After we

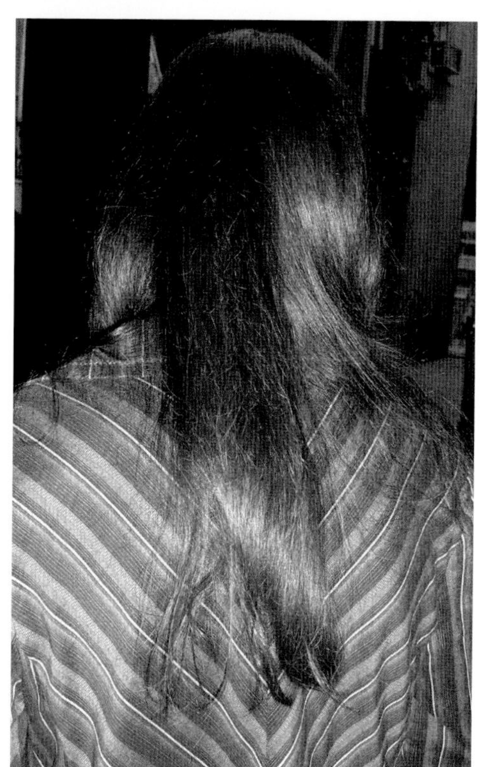

Zooey Deschanel
The Happening, 2008

wrapped most nights, I had enough of the tequila shots with the twenty-somethings. Waking up to go to work only a few hours after I had gone to sleep, after consecutive nineteen-hour days, and the more frequent funerals I was attending began to convince me that I could not keep on doing what I was doing forever.

The death of someone we shared moments and memories with has a morose way of calling attention to our mortality. By 2018, I had lost my mother, my brother, peers, crew members, and a host of close friends to battles with terminal illness and sudden shocks that were delivered via text messages and phone calls at all hours of the day and night—we even delivered some passings with the flippant fodder of entertainment news shows. The loss of Robin Williams, who I worked with twice on *Nine Months* and *Insomnia*, was a shock to many who saw the comedic persona full of laughter. I had experienced him as someone who could pause the mania and listen intently to stories I told about my family, sharing a common adoration for watching our children grow up. Like the rest of the world, I, too, tried to make sense of suicide, recalling how much joy he had brought so many and how he so personally made sure I smiled one way or another every day he walked into the trailer. It was most likely in those two films that I understood the need for "Depends" when Robin was anywhere near my chair. I found an extra gear in my laughter each time he would pick up a comb and conjure some new voice and character, never the same material, consistently inventive to the point of me asking myself, "How does he come up with this shit?!" Although he has faded from many memories, his spirit was radiant while I was in his presence, and whenever I find that extra bit of guttural laugh, I have to let out one last chuckle for Robin, the man who showed me how to laugh a little harder.

Shortly before the world waved goodbye to Robin Williams, I was deeply saddened to learn of my dear friend, James Gandolfini, leaving life behind too soon. We first worked together near the beginning of his career on *Money for Nothing* and then again on *The Mexican* nearly a decade later. If there was ever anyone who was deeply thankful for the opportunities that moviemaking had given them, it was James. Everyone I worked with would say they were fortunate for this or appreciative of it when they spoke of life-altering changes that fame and fortune had granted them. Still, James held his graces in an almost sacred regard. He was a genuinely caring gentleman, always asking how I was doing before discussing anything to do with himself. There were later nights when we were with a group of friends having an extra cocktail or two, and James was always enveloped in the conversation of others. His fascination with hearing someone tell tales of life and love, the occasional political rant, or just something insignificant but ear tweaking enough was evident he would hang on every word that person spoke as if they were telling the most incredible story ever told. His presence was more prominent than any lens or widescreen could ever capture, his heart even larger. James's big bear arms wrapped around me as we said goodbye for the last time after a night out with friends. It was a hug that would warm my soul forever.

I was nearing my eighth decade on this planet, and like I had told Elvis all those years before, I still felt that I had more to do than make movies. However, it is tough to leave something behind that has become so deeply ingrained in my DNA. I never got bored of what I did for a living, never took a moment for granted, and certainly did not do

Harry Connick Jr., *Little Man Tate*, 1991

Jennifer Aniston, *Office Space*, Austin, Texas, 1999

anything that would be considered routine. Besides my body taking its toll on my psyche and ability, I yearned to accomplish one more thing I felt I had done subconsciously and behind the scenes, but not directly for my benefit and others. That last feat would be to tell my story, lessons learned, and experiences, knowing I could not finish the last chapter unless there was an ending to my career. In the Autumn of 2013, I didn't officially announce my departure, but I quietly informed my union in Los Angeles that I was no longer available for work. No press conference or social media post; I was stepping off the court, walking out the revolving door, and marking "unemployed" on everything that required that box to be checked. There were a few tears, a couple of rushes of anxiety, and a half-dozen regrets, not because I did not do everything I had hoped for on a film set, but knowing that I would miss the camaraderie that comes with standing in line every morning chatting with my peers as we wait for a breakfast burrito at the catering trailer.

Ready to chart my course, sailing into retirement, the golden years on the horizon, the phone rang one afternoon, and I pulled up the anchor and headed back to the dock.

"Come do this movie with me in Atlanta," my dear friend, Jennifer Aniston, pleasantly pleaded on the other end of the line.

Not far enough away from the desire in my bones to make one more movie, recalling all the fun we had on *Office Space* years ago, I said yes and packed my equipment trunks one more time. We filmed *Dumplin'* in the heat of Georgia late in the summer of 2017. Imagine making a movie with the spit, spirit, and spunk of Dolly Parton meandering through the production as her music and persona play as an unseen character everywhere in the script. That made it virtually impossible not to always have a smile on my face, Dolly's music playing in the trailer, and the occasional lit Novena candle with her portrait in glitter paint on the glass for an additional boost of happiness when the humidity outside was stifling. What also made the production special and a way to round out my career was that the Delta Flight Museum was a few miles from our sound stages. We informed them of my presence nearby and that I still had a flight attendant training manual and pill-box hats from my time at the airline. Surprisingly, they did not have these in their archives, and I was invited to privately tour the museum and donate those items in my name. From my first career to my last, I loaded out of the trailer at the end of production and felt I had perfectly completed my life as part of the workforce.

With a tear or two, less anxiety from making ends meet, and zero regrets, I finally started the rest of my life. Those desires to spend more time with friends and family were achieved. Traveling to destinations to enjoy the location rather than live between the sites and attractions opened my eyes to places I had worked in but hadn't yet experienced. I rekindled my love of watching movies, not studying them to see how I could make an actor look different from the rest of their repertoire. I had never understood the term "binge-watching" until I retired, as I rarely had time to catch up on the evening news or episodes of *Days of Our Lives*. I had worked with famous actors for something I had not seen, and the memories of our times together were enriched by watching the entire *Mad Men* series with my buddy, John Hamm, in just a few days. I constantly kept in touch with crew and clients, feeling a little like I was still a part of the whole Hollywood scene but enjoying the view from afar. Baby pictures from those actors who shared desires to start

Bradley Cooper and Julia Roberts, *Valentine's Day*, 2010

a family felt like unrelated grandkids we had spoken about before they were born. Those text messages and phone calls were not about the next film but about the latest experiences of my life, a fulfillment of all the intentions I had worked for my entire life. Seeing those around me achieve those milestones was the greatest reward for waking before dawn and filming beyond sunset.

As I sit with my son and daughter, reliving the lifetime that envelopes the pages in this book, I understand fulfillment in a way that eluded me for far too long. The definition of accomplishment is not defined by money or credits on IMDB but by memories, emotions, and moments of reflection that bring a smile, sometimes a tear, and always a sigh of gratitude that I did exactly what I set out to do in the best way possible. That word continuity meant one thing for every scene I filmed for nearly fifty years: a term for life, love, work, passion, and fortitude as we all strive to navigate our lives daily. I am tipping the needle back to the middle, somewhere between positive and negative in all the circumstances that arrive unannounced at any minute of the day. I do not linger too long in self-absorption, knowing that others need a pick-me-up when they struggle to understand everything. Asking for help or comfort when difficulties arise, appreciative that we have those who care enough to lend an ear when just listening is enough to make us rise to the occasion again. Most of my admiration for people in my life is not what they have achieved with an Oscar, Emmy, or Grammy, but how they brought continuity of life back into balance at the center of the infinite loop more often and with greater ease. That has been the most crucial lesson practiced, not perfected, but ultimately learned and utilized as often as possible.

Further away each day from my last credit rolling up

Robin Williams, *Nine Months*, 1995

Me on the set of the film *Captain Ron,* San Juan, Puerto Rico, 1992

the screen, I occasionally get that little itch under my skin that makes me think I might have just one more movie left in these old bones. The creaking of titanium in my joints mostly drowns out the desire to climb those metal stairs up to my trailer, but a common question still exists. "What movie or actor would be enticement enough to get me back on set?" is often broached by a friend over conversational margaritas. The answer comes quickly on the heels of the inquiry, "Maybe Robert Redford," thinking of those dreamy blue eyes and blond hair I adored from a seat somewhere in the fourth row of the cinema and listened to stories about from colleagues that had the fortune to work with him. A quick scroll through Netflix, a push of the start button, and the man I never met before shows up on my screen as almost any character I can imagine, and those desires to return to my post behind my chair in a trailer somewhere in the middle of nowhere is quickly quelled into fantasy and oblivion. I had the perfect ending to countless scenes of a life that found continuity in every aspect. An encore would only be the cherry on top of a decadent, delicious, and divine dessert from fade in to fade out.

MARTINI IN HAND, IT IS TIME TO BINGE-WATCH THE REST OF LIFE UNFOLDING, OR MAYBE THE FINAL SEASON OF BREAKING BAD.

CHEERS!

FADE OUT:

THANK YOU

Rewind

AL PACINO

To watch you perform is the best gift you could have given me in my career. It was always a pleasure to go to the set and watch your perfectionism come to life.

ANTHONY HOPKINS

Making tacos for you in Virginia was such a fun evening for all of us. Thank you for playing so many different roles—each one is more amazing than the last.

BARBARA HERSHEY

Thank you for giving me one of the best compliments I have ever received in my career. The first time I had you in my chair and I touched your head, you said the minute I did, you knew what kind of a professional hairdresser I was. I will always appreciate your kind words of encouragement when I was going through a difficult time in my life. I wish you the best life that you deserve.

BENECIO DEL TORO

You top the charts as being one of the kindest actors I have worked with. I was honored to do your hair. You so deserved the Oscar you won as the Best Supporting Actor in *Traffic*.

BILL BANNERMAN

What a comfort and how understanding you were when my husband took ill and passed away while working with you. I thank you for your endearing kindness. Your trust in bringing me in to do Kristen Stewart's hair in The Twilight Saga film series was a great honor. I wish you the best, always.

BOB MILLS

Looking back at our beginning of working together and then getting back years later, being able to share and make more films with you is my blast from the past into the future. Watching you as the great make-up artist you are and the professionalism you bring to your craft is something I will always regard as a highlight of my career. My best to you and your lovely family. Thanks, Bob, for being in my life.

BRAD PITT

Thank you for asking me to do your hair on *Mr. & Mrs. Smith*, it was a pleasure also watching you act in *The Mexican* and *Ocean's Eleven* & *Twelve* when I was on set with Julia. You are the kindest man I know. You were always willing to help anybody if their families were in need, were in a crisis, or had an illness—you always asked what you could do to help. Glad you liked my sausage, biscuits, and gravy. Thanks, Brad, for being the good man that you are.

BRUCE WILLIS

Being on *The Kid* and the *Mercury Rising* set was a joy. I enjoyed our conversations about Elvis, as you were always so interested in him. Thank you for opening your home to us and for the incredible Johnnycakes you made for all of us for breakfast. Your kind words have always held a special place in my heart. I think of you and pray for you every day, my friend.

CARLA PALMER

I don't have enough pages in my book to tell you how much you mean to me. We have a long history together, from Dallas to Los Angeles to Austin. I loved sharing the trailer with you, but most of all, I loved your friendship. I love you.

CATHERINE ZETA-JONES

I will never forget your kind words when they were most needed; they meant so much to me in *Ocean's Twelve*. What fun it was, blow-drying half of your beautiful head of hair in *Traffic* so we could get you into makeup. Reuniting in the trailer was also great when I was doing Julia Roberts on *America's Sweethearts*.

CHARLES NEWIRTH

It was such a delight watching your success, from working with you as a production manager in *RoboCop* to executive producer in *America's Sweethearts* and *Mona Lisa Smile*. Your credits have been growing through the years as I have enjoyed watching all those films with memories of working together. I did not doubt your success, as the professionalism and kindness you bring to a film are remarkable. Your marriage to Susan, such a wonderful woman, adds to the person you are.

CHRIS COLUMBUS

Filming with you and your team was one of my favorite moments in my career and life. Heartbreak Hotel in Austin and Nine Months in San Francisco are two of my favorite movie locations and experiences. My best to you and your lovely family.

CHRISTOPHER NOLAN

Thank you for allowing me to watch your directing magic on *Insomnia*. You so deserved the Oscar in 2023 for Best Director. Congratulations!

CLAYTON TOWNSEND

You taught me so much in our films with Oliver Stone. Thank you for your wisdom, and I am so proud to have your name on my resume.

CONNIE BRITTON

Thank you for wanting me to play with your locks of hair every day on *Friday Night Lights*. What fun we had! Thank you for bringing so many exciting roles to the screen.

EDWARD NORTON

Thank you for allowing me to bring your characters to life in two of your films. Your dedication and brilliance are beyond comprehension as well as the kind man you are.

FRAN VEGA

What an incredible team we made together while you took such great care of Julia Robert's wardrobe on all those films. Your creativity and choices never failed to amaze me. We couldn't have had more fun and laughs all those years. Love you, Franny.

FRED GABRIELLI

The best caterer ever! Gosh, we go back to Dallas in the '80s and on locations almost everywhere. I remember coming into your trailer and making Caesar salad for the crew more than once. What fun! Bless you and your family always, my friend.

GARRY MARSHALL

I know you are resting in peace knowing all the accomplishments you acquired during your career. How lucky I was to be a part of *Exit to Eden* and then *Valentine's Day* with Julia Roberts. May you rest in peace, Gary.

GEORGE CLOONEY

Working on *Out of Sight* was a great project, even though I didn't do your hair. It came at a sad time of my life after just losing my husband, but you, without a doubt, added laughter and fun with your fantastic humor that made me realize life and people make a lasting and much-needed difference in healing. What fun times we all had on the Ocean's films! You now have such a beautiful family and deserve every bit of it. Thanks, George, for just being George.

HILARY SWANK

Our friendship sparked immediately, as if in a movie. I wasn't even styling your hair. It deepened every time my hands touched your hair. What fun we had quilting and baking every kind of pie. We have always been there for each other. Watching you study for your roles and perform, there is no doubt in my mind of how deserving you are of your two

Oscars. I know I will see you achieving more because you are so brilliant. And, WOW, you are a natural at being the twins' mommy. Love and thank you, friend.

HORTON FOOTE

What an honor and delight to have worked with you on two of your films. Having you come to the set with your Oscar for *Tender Mercies* was such a thrill. You and your family were more than a joy to always be in the same company. May you rest in peace, Horton.

HUGH GRANT

Thank you, Hugh, for letting me tussle your hair every day on the set of *Nine Months* and trusting me to keep it trimmed.

JAMES GANDOLFINI

What a great loss you have been to the film community and the world. Thank you for allowing us to watch your talent and the kind gentleman you were. Riding the MGM Grand Lazy River in Las Vegas with you was a blast because the waitress was there with our tequila shots every time we passed the starting point. May you rest in peace, James.

JEAN BLACK

What a career you have had as Brad Pitt's makeup artist! Are there any looks left for him? I loved working on *Mr. & Mrs. Smith* as a team with you and *The Twilight Saga: Breaking Dawn*. My only regret is not sharing the makeup trailer with you on more films. The ones we did do were some of the best because of you. But most of all, my Texas friend, you mean the world to me, and so does your family. Thank you for continuing our friendship. Love you, Jean.

JENNIFER ANISTON

Office Space was such a fun film to do your locks on, and Austin was a great place to film. Your kindness toward everyone, especially toward me, was always extraordinary.

Not only that, but I was honored a year after retiring when you asked me to do *Dumplin'*, and it was such a fun film. Most of all, your professionalism and the fun and laughs you brought to the set never made it seem like a job. You deserve the best life because of the actress and the woman you are. Thank you for being in my life.

JENNIFER JAHANBIGLOO

The best colorist ever. Thank you for perfectly coloring many of my actors' and actresses' hair. Whether it was on location or in your salon, you were such a big part of many of my films. Thank you, my f riend.

JENNIFER LOPEZ

What a pleasant surprise you chose me to do your hair for *Out of Sight with* George Clooney. I had the time of my life creating all those different styles on your beautiful head of hair. Your professionalism and down-to-earth personality were a joy to work with. You deserve all the success you have accomplished in your music and movie roles. Thank you, thank you, thank you.

JOE ROTH

You gave Hollywood a palpable gift by moving to California, joining the top ranks of producers, managing a major studio, and directing films. How do I ever thank you for the opportunity to be a part of your films like *America's Sweethearts*, *Snow White and the Huntsman*, and *Mona Lisa Smile*, and for our countless conversations while cutting your hair? I will always cherish the inspiration you gave me, my kind friend.

JOHN CUSACK

I've always admired your patience when we did so much to your hair on *Money for Nothing*. It was great being reunited with you on *America's Sweethearts*. Even though I didn't do your hair, visiting with you was a pleasure. My best to you always.

JOHN HUGHES

My deepest gratitude, and what a pleasure it was to work with you. *Curly Sue* was John's last directorial film, but his list of writings has all of our hearts. Spending half a year in Chicago for that film was one of my favorite locations and experiences of my entire career. May you rest in peace, John.

JONATHAN LYNN

Thank you for your fine directions, which I participated in on Sgt. Bilko and Greedy. Most of all, thank you for your kindness and words when I lost my husband. Best to you, always.

JODIE FOSTER

Watching you direct *Little Man Tate* and then seeing you step in front of the camera to become the fabulous actress you are was a challenge, but you pulled it off beautifully. You taught me how smoothly one could run a set in both areas. You taught me the love of tequila at our wrap parties. You continue to amaze me as I watch you in many films.

JULIANNE MOORE

What fun we had in San Francisco filming *Nine Months*. Your gorgeous head of hairmade my job easier. I am grateful we can continue watching the brilliant roles you bring to the screen. Thank you, Julianne.

JULIA ROBERTS

W-O-W... how proud I have always been that not only were you such an essential part of my career, but that we developed a friendship with each film. All the fun times of cooking and baking throughout the years with you had showed me the correct way to cook a turkey. On the first day, we did a hair test for *Erin Brockovich*, and you told me how much you loved sausage, biscuits, and gravy. Later, on *Oprah*, you mentioned how much you loved my sausage, biscuits, and gravy. I carried my recipe to every film and social gathering—once, I hit a record of 20 pounds of sausage and 200 biscuits.

I don't just admire you as an actress; I also admire you as the wife and mother you are. I love you.

KEANU REEVES

From the first time I watched you act on the set of *Tune in Tomorrow* and saw the wonderful young man you were to the successful person you have become in your chosen career, it brings joy to my soul. It was an honor to work with you decades later in Vancouver on *The Day the Earth Stood Still* and to see how humble you have always stayed through the years. Blessings to you, always.

KEVIN COSTNER

How kind you were on *JFK* when doing your hair when I took over for Ellie. Your project choices have shown what a wonderful actor, director, and producer you are, and I wish you the best always. "See you at the Movies."

KRISTEN STEWART

I've always admired you immensely for your diverse film choices. The fun we had cooking in Canada, London, and Louisiana in our kitchens is so memorable, especially when you decided we would bake hundreds of cookies for the crew at Christmas time and put them in their own individually named boxes—quite the undertaking. Tequila was our dear friend when they called it a wrap all those nights. I thank you, my friend, for our shared memories.

KURT RUSSELL

Thank you for all the fun and laughter on *Captain Ron*. It never felt like work. I loved our conversations every day with Martin, and I enjoyed preparing both of your lunches the night before and serving you on your yacht in the ocean at lunchtime every day. Thank you for being such a kind man.

MARTIN SHORT

Could I have had more laughs on a film doing your hair on

Captain Ron? No! Sharing our birthdays together in Puerto Rico on location was one of the best parties ever. Keep us laughing always.

MICHAEL J. FOX

How lucky I was to do your hair on *Poison Ivy* and *Greedy*. What fun we had. I admire all of your accomplishments and know you will continue on your journey in the most respective ways.

NAIMIE

From the '60s throughout the years, it has always been great coming into Naimie's for all the supplies for every film I have done. You always had everything I needed, as did all the makeup artists. Your support for me at different times in my life was more than comforting. My best to your wonderful family, always.

NANCY SINATRA

Nancy, how fortunate I was to do your hair with Elvis on *Speedway* and your TV special as well. Working with your dear father, Frank, and the rest of the guys—Dean Martin, Sammy, and Frank Junior—was more than a highlight of my career. Most of all, being invited to Priscilla Presley's baby shower and to rub her stomach as you were set on carrying out an old Italian wives' tale was the month I was able to conceive. So, thank you, always, for everything.

NATALIE PORTMAN

Thank you for the big surprise when you walked into the makeup trailer one day with a giant stuffed dog for me to hug and sleep with in my empty bed after my husband passed away. To this day, thanks to you, my movie-watching is full of your excellent performances.

OLIVER STONE

Ollie, my thanks for teaching and showing me how real movies are made with the organization of a huge team. Thank you for allowing me the opportunity to list your films on my resume.

RICHARD DEAN

What a wonderful partner you were on set and in the makeup trailer as Julia Roberts' makeup artist. Could we have had any more laughs over dinner and crazy times? No! I love you, my dear GH.

RITA PARILLO

My partner in crime on so many films. Not only the excellent hairdresser you are but the organizer you were in our department. Thank you for always having my back amidst the laughs and fun we shared. Love you, my friend.

ROBERT PATTINSON

Sharing all those months on The Twilight Saga films was fantastic. Working with Kristen, but your being there has always been rewarding to me. Cooking for you and experiencing many restaurants in Canada and London was a collection of memories I will always cherish. I wish you and your family the best of life.

ROBERT WAGNER

From working on *It Takes a Thief* to years later on *Hart to Hart*, your class and wit have never altered. Seeing you in the makeup chair while I was on the other end doing Stephanie Powers' hair was always a pleasure.

SERGE NORMANT

What a pleasure and gift you gave me by being in your company. You always welcomed help and suggestions, and you are the best. Thank you, my friend.

STEFANIE POWERS

Our friendship has continued since the '60s with our annual Christmas cards and notes. After the TV series *The Girl from U.N.C.L.E.*, it was so kind of you to ask me to do a couple of *Hart to Hart* shows. Memories of being in your home and watching you raise so many pets were a joy. I was so excited to run into you in LA a few years back, and it was so much fun catching up. It was like we never lost time. Thank you for fulfilling my life and continuing to do so. Love you.

STEVEN SODERBERGH

Steven Soderbergh—the genius you are. Thank you for always trusting me with each film I did with you. Watching you direct, operating the camera, and constantly multi-tasking, you somehow never ran short of perfection.

ROBIN WILLIAMS

Thank you for the many laughs you gave us working on *Nine Months* and *Insomnia*. Every day was a joy to go to the set. Also, the brilliance you brought to Insomnia was that you were an actor and allowed those in your company to experience your humor and kindness, like winning the lottery. May you rest in peace, Robin.

TIM ALLEN

I don't know if I have enough paper to list how I feel about you and your family. Being part of *The Santa Clause 2, The Shaggy Dog, and Wild Hogs* was so creative and challenging. You probably didn't even realize the kindest words I'd never forget when I came to dinner in your home with your family, and you walked me out to my car at the end of the evening and said, "Never go out of our lives." That has always stayed with me. Watching your girls grow into the young ladies they are has been a pleasure. I don't want to forget Janie, your beautiful, creative wife, who is also so giving, lovely, and intelligent. Thank you, Tim, for never going out of my life.

TOM ARNOLD

Thank you for your support when my husband was so sick and for being at the hospital and offering so much to my family. The comfort you gave us after his passing was so kind of you. It was so great working with you on McHale's Navy as well. Thank you for your kindness, Tom.

TONY GOLDWYN

I was thrilled to think I got my start at MGM when I got the call that you would be directing Hilary Swank in *Conviction*. I couldn't believe that I would be filming with a younger Goldwyn all these years later. You have so many gifts; being listed in the credits was a pleasure.

ZOOEY DESCHANEL

You have the most beautiful hair to work on. What fun we had in Philly when we saw Johnny Mathis on opening night with the Philadelphia Orchestra, our weekends of vintage shopping, and everything we've shared. Thank you for continuing our friendship outside of work with lunches, shopping, and now through texting. Watching you raise your two beautiful children has been a gift. Thank you for being my friend.

MUA/HAIRSTYLIST UNION BROTHERS AND SISTERS

Thank you for being proud members of our organization. To all those who taught me to become a better hairstylist in many ways, I admire all of you and the professionalism you bring to moviemaking. My most profound admiration and thanks.

ACADEMY OF MOTION PICTURE ARTS AND SCIENCES

It is an absolute honor to be a member of this prestigious organization. Being able to vote each year is a highlight of my career. It was such a thrill to go to the Awards a couple of times and enjoy Wolfgang Puck's dinner. I'll never forget it.